# How to be a Marketing Genius

Scientific Advertising
Revisited & Revitalized for Today

# Tony Melvin

**How to be a Marketing Genius - Scientific Advertising Revisited and Revitalized for Today**

*Published by*
**Tony Melvin**
tonymelvin.com

Copyright © 2015, 2017 Tony Melvin
All Rights Reserved.

No part of this book may be reproduced without the permission of the copyright owner.

Disclaimer
The author and publisher expressly disclaim all and any liability to any person, whether a purchaser of this publication or not, in respect of anything and of the consequences of anything done or omitted to be done by any such person in reliance, whether whole or partial, upon the whole or any part of the contents of this publication.

# Contents

Introduction ... 1
Back In Time ... 7

## Part One: Scientific Advertising ... 11
1 - How Advertising Laws Are Established ... 13
2 - Just Salesmanship ... 25
3 - Offer Service ... 35
4 - Mail Order Advertising - What It Teaches ... 41
5 - Headlines ... 53
6 - Psychology ... 63
7 - Being Specific ... 75
8 - Tell Your Full Story ... 81
9 - Art In Advertising ... 91
10 - Things Too Costly ... 97
11 - Information ... 103
12 - Strategy ... 109
13 - Use of Samples ... 115
14 - Getting Distribution ... 125
15 - Test Campaigns ... 133
16 - Leaning On Dealers ... 141
17 - Individuality ... 145
18 - Negative Advertising ... 149
19 - Letter Writing ... 153
20 - A Name That Helps ... 161
21 - Good Business ... 165

## Part Two: Scientific Advertising Applied Today ... 169
22 - Websites ... 171
23 - Landing Pages ... 179
24 - Video Marketing ... 185
25 - 114 Profitable Laws of Advertising & Marketing ... 191
26 - About Tony ... 205

Ever wasted money on ineffective advertising or marketing?

I wrote this for you.


oOo

# Acknowledgements

As always, a book is a team effort. Sonya "the Queen" Houghton not only worked diligently on getting this book published but also brought to life the illustrated Marketing Laws. The enthusiasm of Dustin Anderson is utterly contagious, if this book hits the best-sellers list, it will be in no small part to his altruistic contribution. I thank you both for your dedication and friendship.

All of my books are made an easy read through the careful and considerate work of my wife, Tina, thank you once again for your support and love.

- Tony Melvin

April 2015

# INTRODUCTION

IF YOU HAVE ever wasted money on advertising or marketing, you need to read this book.

If your livelihood depends on attracting customers and making sales, again—you need to read this book.

This is not a plea. It simply good advice, because this book contains *the* answers to successful advertising and marketing.

I have enjoyed success in business and many consider me a "Marketing Genius." That is not a title I have given myself, it is one gained purely through results. Rarely a week goes by without someone asking for my opinion on some aspect of their marketing.

My first teacher in this field was Claude Hopkins and his book *Scientific Advertising*, written in 1923! Yet, despite its age, it contains timeless principles that *everyone in business* and anyone involved in advertising or marketing should know.

Although you have never met Claude, I'm willing to bet that your life has been influenced by him. Let's put that to the test: Back in 1911 the owner of *B. J. Johnson Soap Co.*, B. J. and his newly appointed Sales Manager, Charles Pearce, approached Claude with the view of selling a laundry detergent. Claude and his team advised against it. When Claude asked, "Do you have anything else to sell?"

## Introduction

B.J. replied, "Only toilet soap" which he considered an unprofitable product line. However, Claude convinced them to put $700 for a test campaign. Instead of calling it "Toilet Soap" Claude employed the concept of using a name that *tells a story*. After researching the product, he discovered the ingredients included palm and olive oils, so he coined the name *Palmolive!* That test campaign sparked others, making Palmolive household name. That's the history of the current-day multi-billion company: *Colgate-Palmolive*.

How about another test? Perhaps you have driven a car with Goodyear tires? That too was a brand built by Claude in the early nineteen hundreds.

As Claude openly admits, advertising is not a special talent, restricted to a select "lucky" few. It is a science which can be taught and learned.

In *Part One* of this book I have revisited Claude's works, which are contained here in full and without alteration. My additions include isolating and making clear the Scientific Laws which Claude discovered. Where appropriate, I have simplified the concept and added "How to apply today" information at the end of certain chapters.

*Part Two* of this book explains how to apply these Laws to the online world of websites, advertising and social media.

## Advertising & Marketing

It's worth pointing out that although the title of this book includes the word "Advertising," it's scope is far more reaching. These laws apply to marketing as a whole.

## Introduction

This includes not just paid advertising, but flyers, brochures, websites, business cards, uniforms, letters, posters—everything and anything that promotes your products or services is encompassed in that word "Advertising."

These laws apply to all those areas. They were developed "on-the-job" and not in a classroom or university. They are based on results in the real world. And that is why I called them the *Profitable Laws of Advertising & Marketing*.

I've created an illustrated chart of all the laws and separated them into useful categories. The chart can be downloaded for free from my site.

## Advertising Today

The Wright Brothers—who built and flew the world's first successful airplane in 1903—developed some of the basic laws of aviation. Today, I'm sure that those basic laws of aviation are being used to develop space travel. To help Man reach greater heights.

It's much the same with this text. Claude, through many years of trial and error, developed the *Laws of Advertising*. This book takes those laws and applies them to the modern day world of the internet, Google Adwords and advertising on social media networks such as Facebook, LinkedIn and Twitter—all in the hope that it helps you soar to greater heights in your business or chosen career.

Just as space travel would have been an impossible feat without the prior knowledge and experience of the *Laws of Aviation*, I too would not have been able to complete this task without Claude's fine work.

## The Dark Ages

Many of the laws are based on the results achieved in door-to-door sales techniques and Mail Order advertising—and when developing an exact scientific approach to anything, results *should be* the guiding factor.

Today advertisers receive awards for their ads, which is rather strange. This is a bit like an athlete receiving a trophy based on their costume, rather than their performance. It shows just how much advertising has gone astray. The ultimate purpose of advertising is to sell. Yet advertisers today prefer to bask in the glory of an award winning ad, voted on by other advertisers, rather than report on the actual results (the sales or leads generated by such an ad) for that is the only vote that counts.

More and more, advertising is trying to entertain rather than entice a prospect to make contact. I'm sure you'll find it comical that Claude writes of coming out of the dark ages and into the modern era of advertising more than ninety years ago! And yet here we are, in a darker, more ignorant time than Claude's day—as far as advertising is concerned.

I think Claude would shake his head in wonder at the advertising antics of our "modern age." But I also believe that Claude would be a very wealthy man today as he was, in his time, earning in excess of $185,000 per year in 1907 as an employee of the advertising firm *Lord & Thomas* (that's more than $25.7 million in today's money[1]). And you too can be wealthy applying the techniques in this book. It is not hard to become a genius and achieve

## Introduction

outstanding results when surrounded by such ignorance.

Claude said it himself …

*"Groping in the dark in this field has probably cost enough money to pay the national debt. That is what has filled the advertising graveyards. That is what has discouraged thousands who could profit in this field. And the dawn of knowledge is what is bringing a new day in the advertising world."*

And that is the purpose of this book; to bring business owners and anyone involved with advertising and marketing, out of the "dark ages" and into a Golden Age where every dollar spent on advertising and marketing produces multiple in return.

I speak from experience here, having achieved business success such as: growing an accounting firm from a turnover of $2.5 million to $10 million in 2 years; expanding a publication business from $300,000 to $2 million in 12 months; establishing an online business; success in an international consulting firm and building a national franchise business—in short, success in a wide range of fields, locations and economic climates. What is impressive is not so much the list of different activities I've been involved in, or the results, it's the fact that all of this was done with profitable advertising—simply because I know and apply the Laws contained in this book. Furthermore, knowing these laws has allowed me to live and work whenever and wherever I please.

## Introduction

To be a success in business, you need to know how to sell. To sell, you need clients. To attract clients, you need to understand advertising and marketing. And the best way I know how is to study these laws, again and again.

## Free Bonus

To help you learn and implement the Laws in this book, I've created these resources you can download for free:

1. **Illustrated Chart** - Get a copy of all ***114 Profitable Laws of Marketing & Advertising*** in an easy to follow illustrated chart.

2. **Marketing Checklist** - use this to check your marketing to ensure you are applying the laws.

3. **Campaign Evaluator** - Get a copy of my template that I use to measure the the Cost per Lead and Cost per Sale of all marketing campaigns.

To download visit: tonylink.me/genius

---

[1] Source: tonylink.me/MeasuringWorth

# Back In Time

When reading a book written almost one hundred years ago, it is evident that our language has changed. Certain words and phrases are no longer in such common use. Therefore, to aid the reader in understanding, here are some of the unusual words and phrases used by Claude.

## Key or keyed

Throughout the book Claude talks of "keyed advertising."

This refers to the practice of using a specific word in an advertisement to identify the exact advert that generated that particular response. The word "key" refers to the actual word used: For example, it might be a word used in the return address of a coupon. Today we usually refer to it as a "code".

## Keyed Advertising

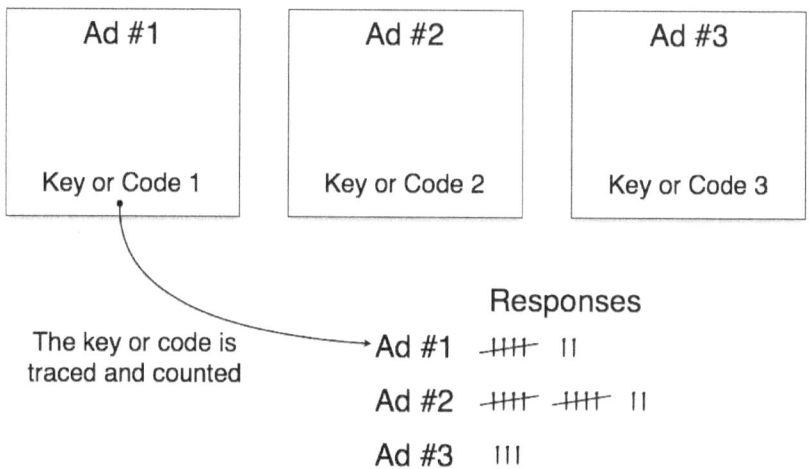

"Keyed advertising" is measured advertising where all of the responses have been traced and counted with the exact result of the ad known. "Unkeyed" is advertising that is not traced and the results are unknown.

## Lines

"Lines" refers to a products or services. Tires is one line. Palmolive soap is another line. Palmolive Shampoo is a different line. The selling of each product line requires a dedicated marketing strategy of its own.

Claude also makes mention of a "line" as an activity or a way of thinking.

## **Uncommon Words**

Throughout this book, I have also taken liberty to define what I consider uncommon words.

This is done by including a simple explanation in parenthesis "( )" following the word being defined. In many cases this does not represent a full and complete definition of the word; it is there as a quick aid for the reader.

I have also added text in brackets "[ ]" to help clarify the meaning of certain phrases or sentences.

I hope that with these words defined and the above clarified you find this book a simple read.

# PART ONE:
# SCIENTIFIC ADVERTISING

### BY CLAUDE HOPKINS

# 1
# How Advertising Laws Are Established

THE TIME HAS come when advertising has in some hands reached the status of a science. It is based on fixed principles and is reasonably exact. The causes and effects have been analyzed until they are well understood. The correct method of procedure have been proved and established. We know what is most effective, and we act on basic laws.

―― FUNDAMENTAL LAW ――
The time has come when advertising has in some hands reached the status of a science. It is based on fixed principles and is reasonably exact.

Advertising, once a gamble, has thus become, under able direction, one of the safest business ventures. Certainly no other enterprise with comparable possibilities need involve so little risk.

Therefore, this book deals, not with theories and opinions, but with well-proved principles and facts. It is written as a textbook for students and a safe guide for advertisers. Every statement has been weighed. The book

## How Advertising Laws Are Established

is confined to establish fundamentals. If we enter any realms of uncertainty we shall carefully denote (indicate) them.

The present status of advertising is due to many reasons. Much national advertising has long been handled by large organizations known as advertising agencies. Some of these agencies, in their hundreds of campaigns, have tested and compared the thousands of plans and ideas. The results have been watched and recorded, so no lessons have been lost.

Such agencies employ a high grade of talent. None but able and experienced men can meet the requirements in national advertising. Working in co-operation, learning from each other and from each new undertaking, some of these men develop into masters.

Individuals may come and go, but they leave their records and ideas behind them. These become a part of the organization's equipment, and a guide to all who follow. Thus, in the course of decades, such agencies become storehouses of advertising experiences, proved principles, and methods.

The larger agencies also come into intimate contact with experts in every department of business. Their clients are usually dominating concerns (businesses). So they see the results of countless methods and policies. They become a clearinghouse for everything pertaining to merchandising (promoting the sale of goods). Nearly every selling question which arises in business is accurately answered by many experiences.

Under these conditions, where they long exist,

advertising and merchandising become exact sciences. Every course is charted. The compass of accurate knowledge directs the shortest, safest, cheapest course to any destination.

―― Fundamental Law ――

The compass of accurate knowledge directs the shortest, safest, cheapest course to any destination.

We learn the principles and prove them by repeated tests. This is done through keyed (measured) advertising, by traced returns, largely by the use of coupons. We compare one way with many others, backward and forward, and record the results. When one method invariably proves best, that method becomes a fixed principle.

Mail order advertising is traced down to the fraction of a penny. The cost per reply and cost per dollar of sale show up with utter exactness.

―― Fundamental Law ――

The cost per reply and cost per dollar of sale show up with utter exactness.

## How Advertising Laws Are Established

One ad is compared with another, one method with another. Headlines, settings (layout), sizes, arguments and pictures are compared. To reduce the cost of results even one percent means much in some mail order advertising. So no guesswork is permitted. One must know what is best. Thus mail order advertising first established many of our basic laws.

In lines (products or services) where direct returns are impossible we compare one town with another. Scores (lots) of methods may be compared in this way, measured by cost of sales.

But the most common way is by use of the coupon. We offer a sample, a book, a free package, or something to induce direct replies. Thus we learn the amount of action which each ad engenders (produces).

—— FUNDAMENTAL LAW ——
We offer a sample, a book, a free package,
or something to induce direct replies.

But those figures are not final. One ad may bring too many worthless replies, another replies that are valuable. So our final conclusions are always based on cost per customer or cost per dollar of sale.

—— FUNDAMENTAL LAW ——
Our final conclusions are always based on
cost per customer or cost per dollar of sale.

These coupon plans are dealt with further in the chapter on "Test Campaigns." Here we explain only how we employ them to discover advertising principles.

In a large ad agency coupon returns are watched and recorded on hundreds of different lines (products and services). In a single line they are sometimes recorded on thousands of separate ads. Thus we test everything pertaining to advertising. We answer nearly every possible question by multitudinous (many) traced returns.

###### —— Fundamental Law ——
We test everything pertaining to advertising.

Some things we learn in this way apply only to particular lines. But even those supply basic principles for analogous (similar) undertakings.

Others [principles learned] apply to all lines. They become fundamentals for advertising in general. They are universally applied. No wise advertiser will ever depart from those unvarying laws.

###### —— Fundamental Law ——
No wise advertiser will ever depart from these fundamental unvarying laws.

We propose in this book to deal with those fundamentals, those universal principles. To teach only established techniques. There is that technique in advertising, as in all art, science and mechanics. And it is, as in all lines (activities), a basic essential.

The lack of those fundamentals has been the main trouble with advertising of the past. Each worker was a law unto himself. All previous knowledge, all progress in the line (activity of advertising), was a closed book to him. It was like a man trying to build a modern locomotive without first ascertaining what others had done. It was like a Columbus starting out to find an undiscovered land.

Men were guided by whims and fancies—vagrant (unpredictable), changing breezes. They rarely arrived at their port. When they did, quite by accident, it was by a long roundabout course.

Each early mariner in this sea mapped his own separate course. There were no charts to guide him. Not a lighthouse marked a harbor, not a buoy showed a reef. The wrecks were unrecorded, so countless ventures came to grief on the same rocks and shoals.

Advertising was a gamble, a speculation of the rashest (reckless) sort. One man's guess on the proper course was as likely to be as good as another's. There were no safe pilots, because few sailed the same course twice.

The condition has been corrected. Now the only uncertainties pertain to people and to products, not to methods. It is hard to measure human idiosyncrasies, the preferences and prejudices, the likes and dislikes that exist. We cannot say that an article will be popular, but we know how to sell it in the most effective way.

Ventures may fail, but the failures are not disasters. Losses, when they occur, are but trifling (unimportant or trivial). And the causes are factors which has nothing to do with the advertising.

Advertising has flourished under these new conditions. It has multiplied in volume, in prestige and respect. The perils have increased many fold. Just because the gamble

## How Advertising Laws Are Established

has become a science, the speculation [is now] a very conservative business.

These facts should be recognized by all. This is no proper field for sophistry (falsehoods) or theory, or for any other will-o'-the-wisp (something impossible to attain). The blind leading the blind is ridiculous. It is pitiful in a field with such vast possibilities. Success is a rarity, a maximum success an impossibility, unless one is guided by laws as immutable (unchanging) as the law of gravitation.

So our main purpose here is to set down those laws, and to tell you how to prove them for yourself. After them come a myriad (countless number) of variations. No two advertising campaigns are ever conducted on lines (products) that are identical. Individuality is an essential. Imitation is a reproach (disgrace). But those variable things which depend on ingenuity have no place in a text book on advertising. This [book] is for groundwork only.

Our hope is to foster (encourage or develop) advertising through a better understanding. To place it on a business basis. To have it recognized as among the safest, surest ventures which lead to large returns.

Thousand of conspicuous (clearly visible) successes show its possibilities. Their variety points out its almost unlimited scope. Yet thousands who need it, who can never attain their deserts (entitled reward) without it, still look upon its accomplishments as somewhat accidental.

That was so, but it is not so now. We hope that this book will throw some new lights on the subject.

## How to Apply Today

Today, measuring the responses and results of your marketing efforts is very easy. Much easier than it was in Claude's day. Prospects can be sent to a website, to complete an online form that automatically tracks responses. You can also track the number of phone calls by using unique phone numbers in certain ads or promotion.

It is wise to track the initial source of a client, that way you can determine the full effect of a campaign. Prospects do not always purchase immediately and may do so several weeks or months after the initial contact. Knowing this helps gauge the effectiveness of a campaign.

Offering a sample or something for free is also very easy to do.

We call these "bribes" or "gifts" rather than samples. We give away something for free in exchange for their contact details. The bribe can be a free eBook, video, checklist, anything of value. This principle is vital. All promotion must offer something for free. That includes your website, your business cards, the footer of your email —every avenue of promotion should entice people to give you their details. That is the fastest way to build a big and profitable business: collect contact details.

Ideally you should collect name, email, physical address and cell number. This allows you to use all 3 main methods of promotion:

1. Email

2. Cell (Texting)
3. Mail

The benefit of also having the physical address is you can promote via mail even if they unsubscribe from email or texting. The absolute minimum information you must collect is an email address.

## Testing Everything

Website pages and emails can easily be tested using a technique called "split testing."

## How Advertising Laws Are Established

It works this way: You design several versions of your website page. Let's say you have three different version of your main website page with the only difference being the headline. The first visitor who comes to your site will see version 1, the second visitor will see version 2 and the third visitor will see version 3. With the fourth visitor, it loops back to version 1 and the fifth visitors see version 2 and so on.

A different version of the website page is automatically displayed for each visitor

The split testing method automatically tallies the responses and provides real-time statistics on which version is the most effective. Many different aspects of your marketing can be tested in this way, providing immediate insight into what is truly driving your prospects.

In short, we can find out what works and what produces the best cost per lead and cost per sale. But the subject of Split Testing could easily fill another book and I want to keep this book on the basics. If want to find out exactly how I do it contact me at tonymelvin.com

# 2
# Just Salesmanship

To properly understand advertising or to learn even its rudiments (basics) one must start with the right conception (idea). Advertising is salesmanship. Its principles are the principles of salesmanship. Successes and failures in both lines are due to like causes. Thus every advertising question should be answered by the salesman's standards.

Let us emphasize that point. The only purpose of advertising is to make sales. It is profitable or unprofitable according to its actual sales.

—— Law ——
The only purpose of advertising is to make sales.

It is not for general effect. It is not to keep your name before the people. It is not primarily to aid your other salesmen. Treat it as a salesman. Force it to justify itself. Compare it with other salesmen. Figure its cost and result. Accept no excuses which good salesmen do not make. Then you will not go far wrong.

## Just Salesmanship

—— Law ——
Advertising is not for general effect.
It is not to keep your name before the people.

The difference is only in degree. Advertising is multiplied salesmanship. It may appeal to thousands while the salesman talks to one. It involves a corresponding cost. Some people spend $10 per word on an average advertisement. Therefore every ad should be a super-salesman.

A salesman's mistake may cost little. An advertisers mistake may cost a thousand times that much. Be more cautious, more exacting, therefore.

A mediocre salesman may affect a small part of your trade. Mediocre advertising affects all of your trade.

Many think of advertising as ad writing. Literary qualifications have no more to do with it than oratory (formal speaking) has with salesmanship.

One must be able to express himself briefly, clearly and convincingly, just as a salesman must. But fine writing is a distinct disadvantage. So is unique literary style. They take attention from the subject. They reveal the hook. Any studies done that attempt to sell, if apparent, creates corresponding resistance.

## Just Salesmanship

That is so in personal salesmanship as in salesmanship-in-print. Fine talkers are rarely good salesmen. They inspire buyers with the fear of over-influence. They create the suspicion that an effort is made to sell them on other lines (methods) than merit.

Successful salesmen are rarely good speech makers. They have few oratorical graces (public speaking manners). They are plain and sincere men who know their customers and know their lines (products). So it is in ad writing.

Many of the ablest men in advertising are graduate salesmen. The best we know have been house-to-house canvassers (someone who sells to people in person). They may know little of grammar, nothing of rhetoric (impressive language), but they know how to use words that convince.

There is one simple way to answer many advertising questions. Ask yourself, "Would it help a salesman sell the goods?" "Would it help me sell them if I met a buyer in person?"

A fair answer to those questions avoids countless mistakes. But when one tries to show off, or does things merely to please himself, he is little likely to strike a chord which leads people to spend money.

## Advertising is Salesmanship-in-print

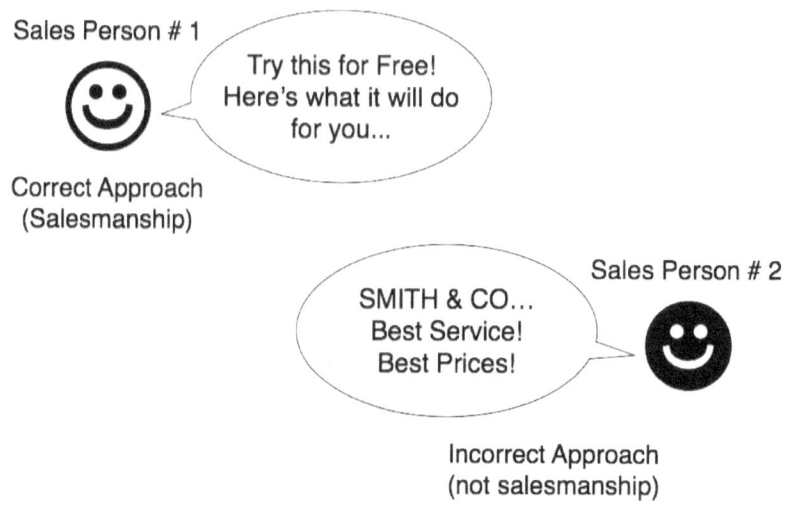

—— Law ——

There is one simple way to answer many advertising questions. Ask yourself, "Would it help a salesman sell the goods?" "Would it help me sell them if I met a buyer in person?" A fair answer to those questions avoids countless mistakes.

Some argue for slogans, some like clever conceits (fancy expressions). Would you use them in personal salesmanship? Can you imagine a customer whom such things would impress? If not, don't rely on them for selling in print.

Some say "Be very brief. People will read for little." Would you say that to a salesman? With a prospect standing before him, would you confine him to any certain number of words? That would be an unthinkable handicap.

So in advertising. The only readers we get are people whom our subject interests. No one reads ads for amusements, long or short. Consider them as prospects standing before you, seeking for information. Give them enough to get action.

―― Law ――

Consider them as prospects standing before you, seeking for information. Give them enough to get action.

Some advocate large type and big headlines. Yet they do not admire salesmen who talk in loud voices. People read all they care to read in 8-point type. Our magazines and newspapers are printed in that type. Folks are accustomed to it. Anything louder is like loud conversation. It gains no attention worthwhile. It may not be offensive, but it is useless and wasteful. It multiplies the cost of your story. And to many it seems loud and blatant.

Others look for something queer (strange) and unusual. They want ads distinctive in style or illustration. Would you want that in a salesman? Do not men who act and dress in normal ways make a far better impression?

Some insist on dressy ads. That is all right to a certain degree, but is quite unimportant. Some poorly-dressed men, prove to be excellent salesmen. Over-dress in either is a fault.

So with countless questions. Measure them by salesmen's standards, not by amusement standards. Ads are not written to entertain. When they do, those entertainment seekers are little likely to be the people whom you want.

That is one of the greatest advertising faults. Ad writers abandon their parts (roles). They forget they are salesmen and try to be performers. Instead of sales, they seek applause.

When you plan or prepare an advertisement, keep before you a typical buyer. Your subject, your headline has gained his or her attention. Then in everything be guided by what you would do if you met the buyer face-to-face. If you are a normal man and a good salesman you will then do your level best (as best you can).

―― LAW ――

When you plan or prepare an advertisement, keep before you a typical buyer and be guided by what you would do if you met the buyer face-to-face.

Don't think of people in the mass. That gives you a blurred view. Think of a typical individual, man or woman, who is likely to want what you sell. Don't try to be amusing. Money spending is a serious matter. Don't boast, for all people resent it. Don't try to show off. Do just what you think a good salesman should do with a half-sold person before him.

###### —— LAW ——
Don't think of people in the mass. That gives you a blurred view. Think of a typical individual, man or woman, who is likely to want what you sell.

Some advertising men go out in person and sell to people before they plan to write an ad. One of the ablest of them has spent weeks on one article, selling from house to house. In this way they learn the reactions from different forms of argument and approach. They learn what possible buyers want and the factors which don't appeal. It is quite customary to interview hundreds of possible customers.

###### —— LAW ——
Before advertising first sell your product or service one-on-one to discover reactions and develop different forms of approach.

Others send out questionnaires to learn the attitude of the buyers. In some way all must learn how to strike responsive chords. Guesswork is very expensive.

###### —— LAW ——
Send out questionnaires to learn the attitude of the buyers.

The maker of an advertised article (product) knows the manufacturing side and probably the dealers' (local retailers') side. But this very knowledge often leads him astray in respect to customers. His interests are not in their interests. The advertising man studies the consumer. He tries to place himself in the position of the buyer. His success largely depends on doing that to the exclusion of everything else.

The advertising man studies the consumer. He tries to place himself in the position of the buyer. His success largely depends on doing that to the exclusion of everything else.

This book will contain no more important chapter than this one on salesmanship. The reason for most of the non-successes in advertising is trying to sell people what they do not want. But next to that comes lack of true salesmanship.

—— LAW ——
The reason for most of the non-successes in advertising is trying to sell people what they do not want.

Ads are planned and written with some utterly wrong conception. They are written to please the seller. The interest of the buyer are forgotten. One can never sell goods profitably, in person or in print, when that attitude exists.

## How to Apply Today

There are a number of ways to survey clients. There are many online apps that provide a simple way to collect information from prospects and clients. I find that offering a simple gift or reward for completing the survey often increases response rates.

Another method of surveying is by using a blog. If you write blog articles on a regular basis, you can immediately see which ones are more popular than others. This provides a simple insight into the minds of your clients. I used this method to decide on the title and topics for events when I was running a national accounting firm in Australia. It proved very successful with crowds over 500 attending and paying $59 per seat.

Also, by encouraging feedback and comments via your blog (or survey) helps you discover the reactions of your prospects. You can do it all without cost. The information gathered can make the difference between a successful campaign and a complete flop. It's well worth doing. (Note that I cover more about website design and SEO in Part Two in the chapter *Websites*)

# 3
## OFFER SERVICE

REMEMBER THE PEOPLE you address are selfish, as we all are. They care nothing about your interests or profit. They seek service for themselves. Ignoring this fact is a common mistake and a costly mistake in advertising. Ads say in effect, "Buy my brand. Give me the trade you give to others. Let me have the money." That is not a popular appeal.

―――― LAW ――――

Remember the people you address are selfish, as we all are. They care nothing about your interests or profit. They seek service for themselves.

The best ads ask no one to buy. That is useless. Often they do not quote a price. They do not say that dealers (local retailers) handle the product.

## Offer Service

The ads are based entirely on service. They offer wanted information. They cite (mention) advantages to users. Perhaps they offer a sample, or to buy the first package [with a voucher], or to send something on approval (try before you buy), so the customer may prove the claims without any cost or risks.

Some of these ads seem altruistic (selfless, more concerned with others). But they are based on the knowledge of human nature. The writers know how people are led to buy.

Here again is salesmanship. The good salesman does not merely cry a name. He doesn't say, "Buy my article." He pictures the customer's side of his service until the natural result is to buy.

—— Law ——

The best ads ask no one to buy. The ads are based entirely on service. They offer wanted information. They mention advantages to users. Perhaps they offer a sample, or to buy the first package, or to send something on approval, so the customer may prove the claims without any cost or risks.

A brush maker has some 2,000 canvassers (salesmen) who sells brushes from house to house. He is enormously successful in a line which would seem very difficult. And it would be for his men if they asked the housewives to buy.

## Offer Service

But they don't. They go to the door and say, "I was sent here to give you a brush. I have samples here and I want you to take your choice."

The housewife is all smiles and attention. In picking out one brush she sees several she wants. She is also anxious to reciprocate the gift. So the salesman gets an order.

Another concern (business) sells coffee, etc., by wagons in some 500 cities. The man drops in with a half-pound of coffee and says, "Accept this package and try it. I'll come back in a few days to ask how you liked it."

Even when he comes back he doesn't ask for an order. He explains that he wants the women to have a fine kitchen utensil. It isn't free, but if she likes the coffee he will credit five cents on each pound she buys until she has paid for the article (kitchen utensil). Always some service.

The maker of the electric sewing machine motor found advertising difficult. So, on good advice, he ceased soliciting a purchase. He offered to send to any home, through any dealer, a [sewing machine] motor for one weeks' use. With it would come a man to show how to operate it. "Let us help you for a week without cost or obligation," said the ad. Such an offer was resistless, and about nine in ten of the trials led to sales.

So in many, many lines. Cigar makers send out boxes to anyone and say, "Smoke ten, then keep them or return them, as you wish."

Makers of books, typewriters, washing machines, kitchen cabinets, vacuum sweepers, etc., send out their products without any prepayment. They say, "Use them a week, then do as you wish." Practically all merchandise

## Offer Service

sold by mail is sent subject to return.

These are all common principles of salesmanship. The most ignorant peddler (salesman) applies them. Yet the salesman-in-print very often forgets them. He talks about his interest. He blazons (displays obviously) a name, as though that was of importance. His phrase is, "Drive people to the stores," and that is his attitude in everything he says.

People can be coaxed but not driven. Whatever they do they do to please themselves. Many fewer mistakes would be made in advertising if these facts were never forgotten.

——— LAW ———
People can be coaxed but not driven.
Whatever they do they do to please themselves.
Fewer mistakes would be made in advertising
if these facts were never forgotten.

## How to Apply Today

Offering something for free is vital. All of your promotion should do so. There is a simple rule when it comes to business: *The bigger your list, the more money you make and the more your business is worth.* By "list" I mean your contact list of both prospects and clients.

Offering something for free is a way to select out those who want to listen to your message. Prominently display your free gift or bribe on your website, make them stand out. Don't ask visitors to "join our mailing list" or "subscribe to a free newsletter" that is like offering somebody cardboard for breakfast. It has absolutely no

## Offer Service

appeal. Your bribe or gift must be something of value to them, it works best when it provides an instant cure to a problem they have right now. It can be as simple as a "Download our 3 point checklist to solve _ (insert problem)."

All promotion should offer such a gift. Even your business card which, for many, has wasted space on the back. Promote your free gift there and build your list!

# 4
# Mail Order Advertising - What It Teaches

The severest test of an advertising man is in selling goods by mail. But that is a school from which he must graduate before he can hope for success. There cost and result are immediately apparent. False theories melt away like snowflakes in the sun. The advertising is profitable or it is not, clearly on the face of returns. Figures which do not lie tell one at once the merits of an ad.

This puts men on their mettle (tests someone's ability to cope with difficulties). All guesswork is eliminated. Every mistake is conspicuous (clearly visible). One quickly loses his conceit (pride) by learning how often his judgment errs —often nine times in ten.

There one learns that advertising must be done on a scientific basis to have any fair chance of success. And he learns that every wasted dollar adds to the cost of results.

Here is a tough efficiency and economy under a master who can't be fooled. Then, and only then, is he apt to apply the same principles and keys (measurements) to all advertising.

A man was selling a five-dollar article (product). The

# Mail Order Advertising - What It Teaches

replies from his ad cost him 85 cents. Another man submitted an ad which he thought better. The replies cost $14.20 each. Another man submitted an ad which for two years brought replies at an average of 41 cents each.

Consider the difference on 250,000 replies per year. Think how valuable was the man who cut the cost in two. Think what it would have meant to continue that $14.20 ad without any key (measurement) on returns.

## Advertising Results

| Cost of Replies | Cost to Generate 250,000 Replies |
| --- | --- |
| $0.85 | $212,500 |
| $14.20 | $3,550,000 |
| $0.41 | $102,500 |

Yet there are thousands of advertisers who do just that. They spend large sums on a guess. And they are doing what that man did—paying for sales from 2 to 35 times [more than] what they need [to] cost.

A study of mail order advertising reveals many things worth learning. It is a prime subject for study. In the first place, if continued, you know what pays. It is therefore good advertising as applied to that line (product or service).

The probability is that the ad has resulted from many traced comparisons. It is therefore the best advertising yet discovered for that line.

Study those ads with respect. There is proved advertising, not theoretical. It will not deceive you. The lessons it teaches are principles which wise men apply to all advertising.

Mail order advertising is always set (laid out) in small type (font). It is usually set in smaller type than ordinary print. That economy of space is universal. So it proves conclusively that larger type does not pay.

Remember that when you double your space by doubling the size of your type. The ad may still be profitable. But traced returns have proved that you [are] paying a double price for sales.

In mail order advertising there is no wasted space. Every line is utilized. Borders are rarely used. Remember that when you are tempted to leave valuable space unoccupied.

—— LAW ——
In advertising there is no wasted space.
Every line is utilized.

## Mail Order Advertising - What It Teaches

In mail order advertising there is no palaver (unnecessary talk). There is no boasting, save of super-service. There is no useless talk. There is no attempt at entertainment. There is nothing to amuse.

—— Law ——
In advertising there is no useless talk.
There is no attempt at entertainment.
There is nothing to amuse.

Mail order advertising usually contains a coupon. That is there to cut out as a reminder of something the reader has decided to do.

Mail order advertisers know that readers forget. They are reading a magazine of interest. They may be absorbed in a story. A large percentage of people who read an ad and decide to act will forget that decision in five minutes. The mail order advertiser knows that waste by tests, and he does not propose to accept it. So he inserts that reminder to be cut out, and it turns up when the reader is ready to act.

In mail order advertising the pictures are always to the point. They are salesmen in themselves. They earn space they occupy. The size is gauged by their importance. The picture of a dress one is trying to sell may occupy much space. Less important things get smaller spaces.

—— Law ——
In advertising the pictures are always to the point.
They are salesmen in themselves.

## Mail Order Advertising - What It Teaches

They the earn space they occupy.

Pictures in ordinary advertising may teach little. They probably result in whims (sudden, unexplained impulses). But pictures in mail order advertising may form half the cost of selling. And you may be sure that everything about them has been decided by many comparative tests.

Before you use useless pictures, merely to decorate or interest, look over some mail order ads. Mark what their verdict is.

A man advertised an incubator to be sold by mail. Type ads with right headlines brought excellent returns. But he conceived the idea that a striking picture would increase those returns. So he increased his space 50 percent to add a row of chickens in silhouette (dark shape).

It did make a striking ad, but his cost per reply was increased by exactly that 50 percent. The new ad, costing one-half more for every insertion, brought not one added sale.

The man learned that incubator buyers were practical people. They were looking for attractive offers, not for pictures.

Think of the countless untraced campaigns where a whim of that kind costs half the advertising money without a penny in return. And it may go on year after year.

Mail order advertising tells a complete story if the purpose is to make an immediate sale. You see no limitations there are on amount of copy.

The motto there is, "The more you tell the more you

sell." And it has never failed to prove out so in any test we know.

—— Law ——
The more you tell the more you sell.

Sometimes the advertiser uses small ads, sometimes large ads. None are too small to tell a reasonable story. But an ad twice larger brings twice the returns. A four times larger ad brings four times the returns, and usually some in addition.

## How Ad Size Increases Results

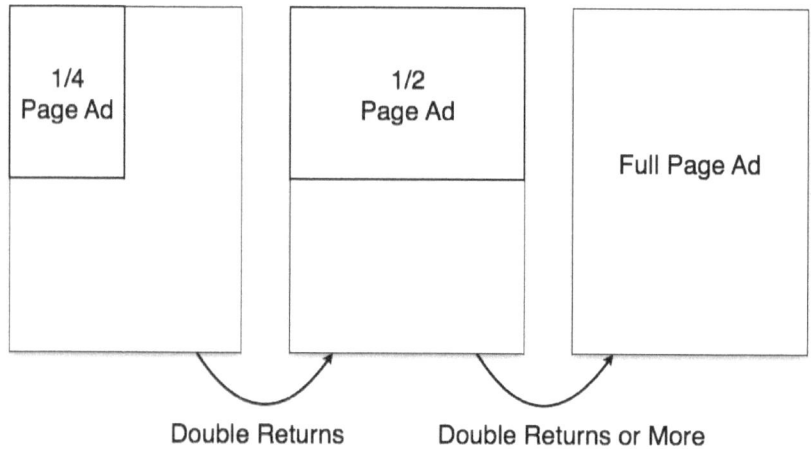

But this occurs only when the larger space is utilized as well as the small space. Set half-page copy in a page space and you double the cost in returns. We have seen many a test prove that.

Look at an ad of the Mead Cycle Company—a typical mail order ad (see below). These have been running for many years. The ads are unchanging. Mr. Mead told the writer that not for $10,000 would he change a single word in his ads.

Source: jimlangley.net

For many years he compared one ad with the other. And the ads you see today are the final results of all those experiments. Note the picture he uses, the headlines, the economy of space, the small type. Those ads are as near perfect for their purpose as an ad can be.

So with any other mail order ad which has long continued. Every feature, every word and picture teaches advertising at its best. You may not like them. You may say they are unattractive, crowded, hard to read—anything you will. But the test of results has proved those ads the best salesman those lines have yet discovered. And they certainly pay.

Mail order advertising is the court of last resort (final place where judgment is made). You may get the same instruction, if you will, by keying (measuring) other ads. But mail order ads are models. They are selling goods profitably in a difficult way. It is far harder to get mail order than to send buyers to the stores. It is hard to sell goods which can't be seen. Ads which do that are excellent examples of what advertising should be.

We cannot often follow all the principle of mail order advertising, though we know we should. The advertiser forces a compromise. Perhaps pride in our ads has an influence. But every departure from those principles adds to our selling cost. Therefore it is always a question of what we are willing to pay for our frivolities (silliness).

We can at least know what we pay. We can make keyed (measured) comparisons, one ad with another. Whenever we do we invariably find that the nearer we get to proved mail order copy the more customers we get for our money.

—— LAW ——

We compare the results of one ad with another. Whenever we do we invariably find that the nearer we get to proven mail order copy the more customers we get for our money.

This is another important chapter. Think it over. What real difference is there between inducing a customer to order by mail or order from his dealer (local retailer)? Why should the methods of salesmanship differ?

They should not. When they do, it is for one of two reasons. Either the advertiser does not know what the mail order advertiser knows. He is advertising blindly. Or he deliberately sacrifices a percentage of his returns to gratify (satisfy) some desire.

There is some apology for that, just as there is for fine offices and buildings. Most of us can afford to do something for pride and opinion. But let us know what we are doing. Let us know the cost of our pride. Then, if our advertising fails to bring us the wanted returns, let us go back to our model—a good mail order ad—and eliminate some of our waste.

## How to Apply Today

The "no wasted space" law applies, not just to printed ads and promotion, but also to websites. While a website has unlimited "space" there is, however, that all visitors see when they first view your website. We refer to this as the area "above the fold" and it is the most important space on your website. And the laws in this chapter apply to that area.

## Most Value Website Space

All of your effort, all of the content in this section—every image, text or video—should have one purpose only: to persuade the visitor to enter their contact details and claim their free gift. That means you avoid useless images, fancy moving graphics, detailed and complicated menu options. All of these things are distractions. Keep it simple and keep it focused.

Remember this point: Most website designers are just that. They are *designers*, not marketers. In marketing we care about the result, not how it looks. A plain website might create ten times more prospects than a fancy looking website. But you will never know if you don't test. And web designers rarely test.

By applying every law in this chapter (and in the next) to this space on your website, you will start to build your list and your sales pipeline. This advice, if you follow it, has the potential to double your sales.

## **Coupons**

Mailed coupons are not as popular today but many marketers I know still insist that a dotted line around the call-to-action section of an ad produces a better response.

The concept of a coupon is to make it easy for the prospect to order. A modern day method is aptly called the "Quick Response Code." It's more commonly referred to as a *"QR Code"* and is a type of barcode that can be read by smartphone cameras. You can create these QR Code and link them to specific website pages or even initiate calls.

These are becoming increasingly popular and save the prospect time. For someone in a rush they can take a quick photo of the ad and check out the link later.

I've included one below as an example. If you are unsure how to do it then google "how to scan QR code." I find that *Google Goggles* app is the best and its free.

To create your own QR Code visit qr-code-generator.com

# 5
## HEADLINES

THE DIFFERENCE BETWEEN advertising and personal salesmanship lies largely in personal contact. The salesman is there to demand attention. He cannot be ignored. The advertisement can be ignored.

But the salesman wastes much of his time on prospects whom he can never hope to interest. He cannot pick them out. The advertisement is read only by interested people who, by their own volition, study what we have to say.

The purpose of a headline is to pick out people you can interest. You wish to talk to someone in a crowd. So the first thing you say is, "Hey there, Bill Jones" to get the right persons attention.

—— LAW ——

The purpose of a headline is to
pick out people you can interest.

# Headlines

So it is in an advertisement. What you have will interest certain people only, and for certain reasons. You care only for those people. Then create a headline which will hail (call out to) those people only.

What you have will interest certain people only, and for certain reasons. You care only for those people.

Perhaps a blind headline or some clever conceit (fancy expression) will attract many times as many. But they may consist of mostly impossible subjects for what you have to offer. And the people you are after may never realize that the ad refers to something they may want.

Headlines on ads are like headlines on news items. Nobody reads a whole newspaper. One is interested in financial news, one in political, one in society, one in cookery, one in sports, etc. There are whole pages in any newspaper which we may never scan at all. Yet other people might turn directly to those pages.

We pick out what we wish to read by headlines, and we don't want those headlines misleading. The writing of headlines is one of the greatest journalistic arts. They either conceal or reveal an interest.

—— Law ——

We pick out what we wish to read by headlines, and we don't want those headlines misleading.

Suppose a newspaper article stated that a certain

woman was the most beautiful in the city. That article would be of intense interest to that woman and her friends. But neither she nor her friends would ever read it if the headline was "Egyptian Psychology."

So in advertising. It is commonly said that people do not read advertisements. That is silly, of course. We who spend millions in advertising and watch the returns [of money] marvel (are amazed) at the readers we get. Again and again we see 20 percent of all the readers of a newspaper cut out a certain coupon.

But people do not read ads for amusement. They don't read ads which, at a glance, seem to offer nothing interesting. A double-page ad on women's dresses will not gain a glance from a man. Nor will a shaving cream ad from a woman.

Always bear these facts in mind. People are hurried. The average person worth cultivating (winning the friendship or favor of) has too much to read. They skip three-fourths of the reading matter which they pay to get. They are not going to read your business talk unless you make it worth their while and let the headline show it.

—— Law ——

Always bear these facts in mind. People are hurried. The average person worth cultivating has too much to read. They skip three-fourths of the reading matter which they pay to get. They are not going to read your business talk unless you make it worth their while and let the headline show it.

# Headlines

People will not be bored in print. They may listen politely at a dinner table to boasts and personalities, life history, etc. But in print they choose their own companions, their own subjects. They want to be amused or benefited. They want economy, beauty, labor savings, good things to eat and wear. There may be products which interest them more than anything else in the magazine. But they will never know it unless the headline or picture tells them.

—— Law ——
People will not be bored in print or online.

The writer of this chapter (Claude) spends far more time on headlines than on writing. He often spends hours on a single headline. Often scores of headlines are discarded before the right one is selected. For the entire return from an ad depends on attracting the right sort of readers. The best of salesmanship has no chance whatever unless we get a hearing.

—— Law ——
The entire return from an ad depends on attracting the right sort of readers.

The vast difference in headlines is shown by keyed returns which this book advocates. The identical ad run with various headlines differs tremendously in its returns. It is not uncommon for a change in headlines to multiply returns from five or ten times over.

— LAW —

It is not uncommon for a change in headlines to multiply returns from five or ten times over.

So we compare headlines until we know what sort of appeal pays best. That differs in every line, of course.

The writer has before him keyed returns on nearly two thousand headlines used on a single product. The story in these ads are nearly identical. But the returns vary enormously, due to the headlines. So with every keyed return in our record appears the headlines that we used.

## Testing Headlines

Thus we learn what type of headline has the most widespread appeal. The product has many uses. It fosters

## Headlines

beauty. It prevents disease. It aids daintiness (being beautiful or delicate) and cleanliness. We learn to exactness which quality most of our readers seek.

That does not mean we neglect the others. One sort of appeal may bring half the returns of another, yet be important enough to be profitable. We overlook no field that pays. But we know what proportion of our ads should, in the headline, attract any certain class.

For this same reason we employ a vast variety of ads. If we are using twenty magazines we may use twenty separate ads. This [is] because circulations overlap, and because a considerable percentage of people are attracted by each of several forms of approach. We wish to reach them all.

On a soap, for instance, the headline "Keep Clean" might attract a very small percentage. It is too commonplace. So might the headline, "No animal fat." People may not care much about that. The headline, "It floats" might prove interesting. But a headline referring to beauty or complexion might attract many times as many.

An automobile ad might refer in the headline to a good universal joint (a special connection used to transfer power from the motor to the wheels). It might fall flat, because so few buyers think of universal joints. The same ad with a headline, "The Sportiest of Sport Bodies," might out pull the other fifty to one.

This is enough to suggest the importance of headlines. Anyone who keys (measures) ads will be amazed at the difference. The appeals we like best will rarely prove best, because we do not know enough people to average up their desires. So we learn on each line (product or service) by experiment.

But back of all (behind all effective advertising) lie fixed principles. You are presenting an ad to millions. Among them is a percentage, small or large, whom you hope to interest. Go after that percentage and try to strike the chord that responds. If you are advertising corsets, men and children don't interest you. If you are advertising cigars, you have no use for non-smokers. Razors won't attract women, rouge (a red powder or cream used as a cosmetic for coloring the cheeks or lips) will not interest men.

Don't think that those millions will read your ads to find out if your product interests. They will decide at a glance—by your headline or your pictures. Address the people you seek, and them only.

—— LAW ——

Don't think that those millions will read your ads to find out if your product interests. They will decide at a glance—by your headline or your pictures. Address the people you seek, and them only.

## How to Apply Today

The first book I ever wrote had a great title: *How to Legally Reduce Your Tax*. I had become a partner of an Australian accounting firm, and this was part of my marketing strategy. I initially tested the title of the book in headlines for events, so I knew it was going to do well. The result however blew me away. The book became the number one best-selling finance book in the country within three weeks and was the driving force that helped grow that firm from a $2.5 million revenue to $10 million in just two years.

My second book, which I wrote and published six months after the first, was focused on how to invest retirement savings. This book was written for a larger segment of the population and in my opinion had greater potential than the first book. To my surprise and disappointment, the book failed to reach the top 100 best-sellers list. I realized that I didn't thoroughly test the title of the book (truthfully I had gotten a bit lazy with my prior success). So I decided I'd better do some tests and research other books in the same category. In the next print, I changed the title. It then jumped to the top 5 on the best-seller list. That demonstrates the power of testing headlines.

Today, headlines can easily be tested and at much greater speed than in Claude's day. It now takes only days what used to take weeks or months. What used to cost thousands can be done for several hundred. Online advertising platforms such as Google Adwords and Facebook Advertising provide a means to set up different campaigns within hours and get results back within days. It's a marketer's dream.

## Headlines

And it gets better. Using such online platforms, you can define your exact demographic so that your ad will only display to those type of people. For example, you can define gender, location, age and profession to name just a few. This method is so powerful, inexpensive and fast, that I'm sure Claude would faint in disbelief if he could see it in action.

With such tools available to every business owner, from the sole trader to the big corporates, there is no reason to violate the laws in this chapter.

# 6
# PSYCHOLOGY

THE COMPETENT ADVERTISING man must understand psychology (the mental characteristics or attitude of a person or group). The more he knows about it the better. He must learn that certain effects lead to certain reactions, and use that knowledge to increase results and avoid mistakes.

Human nature is perpetual. In most respects it is the same today as in the time of Caesar. So the principles of psychology are fixed and enduring. You will never need to unlearn what you learn about them.

We learn, for instance, that curiosity is one of the strongest human incentives. We employ it whenever we can. Puffed Wheat and Puffed Rice were made successful largely through curiosity. "Grains puffed to 8 times the normal size." "Foods shot from guns." "125 million steam explosions caused in every kernel." (These were headlines used to advertise Quaker's cereals.) These foods were failures before that factor was discovered.

—— LAW ——
We learn that curiosity is one of the

## Psychology

strongest human incentives.

We learn that cheapness is not a strong appeal. Americans are extravagant. They want bargains but not cheapness. They want to feel that they can afford to eat and have and wear the best. Treat them as if they could not and they resent your attitude.

—— Law ——
We learn that cheapness is not a strong appeal.
People want bargains not cheapness.

We learn that people judge largely by price. They are not experts. In the British National Gallery is a painting which is announced in a catalog to have cost $750,000. Most people at first pass it by at a glance. Then later they get farther on in the catalog and learn what the painting cost. They return then and surround it.

—— Law ——
We learn that people judge largely by price
and admire expensive items or service.

A department store advertised at one Easter time a $1,000 hat, and the floor could not hold the women who came to see it.

## Psychology

We often employ this factor in psychology. Perhaps we are advertising a valuable formula. To merely say that would not be impressive. So we state—as a fact—that we paid $100,000 for that formula. That statement when tried has won a wealth of respect.

——— Law ———

When the actual cost of something is promoted, that can impress and attract attention and respect.

Many articles are sold under guarantee—so commonly sold that guarantees have ceased to be impressive. But one concern (business) made a fortune by offering a dealer's (local retailer's) signed warrant (guarantee). The dealer to whom one paid his money agreed in writing to pay it back if asked. Instead of a far-away stranger, a neighbor gave the warrant. The results have led many to try that plan, and it has always proved effective.

Many have advertised, "Try it for a week. If you don't like it we'll return your money." Then someone conceived the idea of sending goods without any money down, and saying, "Pay in a week if you like them." That proved many times more impressive.

## Psychology

One great advertising man stated the difference this way: "Two men came to me, each offering me a horse. Both made equal claims. They were good horses, kind and gentle. A child could drive them. One man said, 'Try the horse for a week. If my claims are not true, come back for your money.' The other man also said, 'Try the horse for a week.' But he added, 'Come and pay me then.' I naturally bought the second man's horse."

Now countless things—cigars, typewriters, washing machines, books, etc.—are sent out in this way on approval. And we find that people are honest. The losses are very small.

An advertiser offered a set of books to business men. The advertising was unprofitable, so he consulted another expert. The ads were impressive. The offer seemed attractive, "But," said the second man, "let us add one little touch which I have found effective. Let us offer to put the buyers name in gilt (gold paint) lettering on each book." That was done, and with scarcely another change in the ads they sold some hundreds of thousands of books. Through some peculiar kink in human psychology it was found that names in gilt gave much added value to the books.

Many send out small gifts, like memorandum (note) books, to customers and prospects. They get very small results. One man sent out a letter to the effect that he had a leather-covered book with a man's name on it. It was waiting on him and would be sent on request.

The form of request was enclosed, and it also asked for certain information. That information indicated lines

# Psychology

(methods) on which a man might be sold.

—— Law ——
Personalization of communication and products often improves response.

Nearly all men, it was found, filled out that request and supplied the information. When a man knows that something belongs to them—something with his name on—he will make an effort to get it, even though the thing is a trifle (thing of little value or importance).

In the same way it is found that an offer limited to a certain class of people is far more effective than a general offer. For instance, an offer limited to veterans of the war. Or to members of a lodge (a branch or meeting place of an organization) or sect (a religious, philosophical or political group). Or to executives. Those who are entitled to any seeming (apparent) advantage will go a long way not to lose that advantage.

—— Law ——
An offer limited to a certain class of people is far more effective than a general offer to everyone.

—— Law ——
Those who are entitled to any seeming (apparent) advantage will go a long way not to lose that advantage.

An advertiser suffered much from substitution (clients buying a similar but different product). He said, "Look out for substitutes," "Be sure you get this brand," etc., with no effect. Those were selfish appeals.

Then he said, "Try our rivals' too"—said it in his headlines. He invited comparisons and showed that he did not fear them. That corrected the situation. Buyers were careful to get the brand so conspicuously superior that its maker could court (risk) a trial of the rest.

Two advertisers offered food products nearly identical. Both offered a full-size package as an introduction. But one gave his package free. The other bought the package. A coupon was good at any store for a package, for which the maker paid retail price.

## Better Way to Offer Something for Free

The first advertiser failed and the second succeeded. The first even lost a large part of the trade he had. He cheapened his product by giving a 15-cent package away. It is hard to pay for an article which has once been free. It is like paying railroad fare after traveling on a pass (not paying).

―― Law ――
Providing the customer with a way to purchase something for free (such as a voucher) is more effective than giving it away for free.

The other gained added respect for his article by paying retail price to let the user try it. An article good enough for the maker to buy is good enough for the user to buy. It is vastly different to pay 15 cents to let you try an article than to simply say "It's free."

So with sampling. Hand an unwanted product to a housewife and she pays it slight respect. She is [in] no mood to see its virtues (benefits). But get her to ask for a sample after reading your story, and she is in a very different position. She knows your claims. She is interested in them, else she would not act. And she expects to find the qualities you told.

―― Law ――
People are naturally interested in a product or service when they know more about it and understand it.

There is a great deal in mental impression. Submit five articles (products) exactly alike and five people may choose one of them. But point out in one some qualities to notice and everyone will find them. The five people then will all choose the same article (product).

If people can be made sick or well by mental impressions, they can be made to favor a certain brand in

## Psychology

that way. And that, on some lines, is the only way to win them.

Two concerns (businesses), side by side, sold women's clothing on installments (payment plans). The appeal, of course, was to poor girls who desire to dress better. One treated them like poor girls and made the bare (simplest or basic) business offer.

The other put a woman in charge [of the shop]—a motherly, dignified, capable woman. They did business in her name. They used her picture. She signed all ads and letters. She wrote to these girls like a friend. She knew herself what it meant to a girl not to be able to dress her best. She had long sought a chance to supply women good clothes and give them all season (suitable time) to pay. Now she was able to do so, with the aid of men (investors) behind her.

There was no comparison in those two appeals. It was not long before this woman's long-established next-door rival had to quit.

—— Law ——
Always maintain rapport with your customers.

The backers (investors) of this [clothing store] business [also] sold house furnishings on installments. Sending out catalogs promiscuously (unselectively, to anybody) did not pay. Offering long-time credit often seems like a reflection (a thing bringing discredit to someone or something).

**Note from Tony:** *Some customers might be offended when offered long-time credit. In other words, they had no way of promoting payment by installments without possibly offending someone. So the*

## Psychology

*approach below was employed instead of the ineffective catalog.*

*In this paragraph below, "Mrs. " refers to the Store Manager mentioned above in the women's clothing store.*

But when a married woman bought garments from Mrs. , and paid as agreed, they [the furnishings store investors] wrote to her something like this: "Mrs. , whom we know, tells us that you are one of her good customers. She has dealt with you, she says, and you do just as you agree. So we have opened with you a credit account on our books, good any time you wish. When you want anything in furnishings, just order it. Pay nothing in advance. We are very glad to send it without any investigation to a person recommended as you are."

That was flattering. Naturally those people, when they wanted some furniture, would order from that house.

There are endless phases to psychology. Some people know them by instinct. Many of them are taught by experience. But we learn most of them from others. When we see one winning method we note it down for use when occasion offers.

These things are very important. An identical offer made in a different way may bring multiplied returns. Somewhere in the mines of business experience we must find the best method somehow.

—— Law ——
An identical offer made in a different way may bring multiplied returns.

Psychology

# How to Apply Today

In addition to testing headlines, pictures and your message there are two other things you should test:

1. The Offer
2. The Price

## Testing the Offer

As Claude states, cheapness is not appealing, but a bargain is. Using this law I have always found it more effective to add value to a product or service instead of discounting it. For example, let's say we're selling shoes. Rather than reduce the cost 25%, keep the price the same and add value by including socks and shoe polish as a bonus. Now the buyer is getting a bargain. That has other benefits too. The value of the bonuses might be $20 yet the actual cost to us might be less than $5. We have also maintained the value of the shoe and its brand by not reducing the price. That is a much better offer.

Here's a real life example of testing different offers. Several years ago many of the banks in Australia started offering "honeymoon" interest rates on home loans. Their offer was to discount the interest rate for the first 12 months. They called this the "honeymoon period." A clever marketer I know was called in to help a small bank increase their market share. The bank was all set to offer a "honeymoon" special but instead he convinced them to do something different: "Why not send them on a honeymoon rather than discount the loan?" The typical saving during the first 12 months was around $5000 so instead of the discount, this bank simply offered a free holiday with every new loan, valued at $5000. With that offer they became one of the top lenders.

## Testing the Price

Testing the price of your product or service is something that not many business owners even consider. I recall one product I worked with, it was a simple product that enabled a person to hang plants from the ceiling. It cost very little to make, but we had no idea what the retail price should be. People had plenty of opinions of course and most settled around the $2.95 price point. But I convinced them to put it to the test in actual stores. We tested different prices from $1.95 to $7.95. We discovered that $4.95 was the price that sold the most.

Often higher prices sell better than lower ones. Also, if you double your price you only need to sell half as much to make the same profit. However, it depends on your marketing strategy and business. When selling products, often the higher the quantity, the less it costs to manufacture. Service type businesses, however, benefit greatly from higher margins and enable one to provide a better service. In short, prices are worth testing in all types of businesses.

# 7
# BEING SPECIFIC

PLATITUDES (OVERUSED, DULL statements) and generalities roll off the human understanding like water from a duck. They leave no impression whatever. To say, "Best in the world," "Lowest price in existence," etc, are at best simply claiming the expected. But superlatives (exaggerations) of that sort are usually damaging. They suggest looseness of expression, a tendency to exaggerate, a careless truth. They lead readers to discount all the statements that you make.

—— LAW ——
Exaggerations are usually damaging. They suggest looseness of expression, a tendency to exaggerate, a careless truth. They lead readers to discount all the statements that you make.

People recognize a certain license in selling talk as they do poetry. A man may say, "Supreme in quality" without seeming a liar, though one may know that the other brands are equally as good. One expects a salesman to put his best foot forward and excuses some exaggeration born of enthusiasm. But just for that reason general statements

## Being Specific

count for little. And a man inclined to superlatives must expect that his every statement will be taken with some caution.

But a man who makes a specific claim is either telling the truth or a lie. People do not expect an advertiser to lie. They know that he can't lie in the best mediums. The growing respect in advertising has largely come through a growing regard for its truth.

So a definite statement is usually accepted. Actual figures are not generally discounted. Specific facts, when stated, have their full weight and effect.

—— LAW ——
Specific facts, when stated,
have their full weight and effect.

This is very important to consider in written or personal salesmanship. The weight of an argument may often be multiplied by making it specific. Say that a tungsten (a type of metal used in lights) lamp gives more light than a carbon and you leave some doubt. Say it gives three and one-third times the light and people realize that you have made tests and comparisons.

A dealer may say, "Our prices have been reduced" without creating any marked impression. But when he says "Our prices have been reduced 25 percent" he gets the full value of his announcement.

A mail order advertiser sold women's clothing to people of the poorer classes. For years he used the slogan, "Lowest prices in America." His rivals all copied that. Then he guaranteed to undersell any other dealer. His

## Being Specific

rivals did likewise. Soon those claims became common to every advertiser in his line, and they became commonplace.

Then under able advice, he changed his statement to "Our net profit is 3 percent." That was a definite statement and it proved very impressive. With their volume of business it was evident that their prices must be minimum. No one could be expected to do business on less than 3 percent. The next year their business made a sensational increase.

At one time in the automobile business there was a general impression that profits were excessive. One well-advised advertiser came out with this statement, "Our profit is 9 percent." Then he cited actual costs on the hidden costs of a $1,500 car. They amounted to $735, without including anything one could easily see. This advertiser made a great success along those lines at that time.

Shaving soaps have long been advertised "Abundant lather," "Does not dry on the face," "Acts quickly," etc. One advertiser had as good a chance as the other to impress those claims.

## Being Specific

Then a new maker came into the field. It was a tremendously difficult field, for every customer had to be taken from someone else. He stated specific facts. He said, "Softens the beard in one minute." "Maintains its creamy fullness for ten minutes on the face." "The final result of testing and comparing 130 formulas." Perhaps never in advertising has there been a quicker and greater success in an equally difficult field.

Makers of safety razors have long advertised quick shaves. One maker advertised a 78-second shave. That was definite. It indicated actual tests. That man at once made a sensational advance in his sales.

In the old days all beers were advertised as "Pure." The claim made no impression. The bigger the type used, the bigger the folly (foolishness). After millions had been spent to impress a platitude (overused, dull statement), one brewer pictured a plate glass (thick, clear glass) room where beer was cooled in filtered air. He pictured a filter of white wood pulp (a type of paper filter) through which every drop was cleared (purified). He told how bottles were washed four times by machinery. How he went down 4,000 feet for pure water. How 1,018 experiments had been made to attain a yeast to give beer that matchless flavor. And how all the yeast was forever made from that adopted mother cell.

All claims were such as any brewer might have made. They were mere essentials in ordinary brewing. But he was the first to tell the people about them, while others cried merely "pure beer." He made the greatest success that was ever made in beer advertising.

"Used the world over" is a very elastic (stretched) claim.

Then one advertiser said, "Used by the peoples of 52 nations," and many others followed.

One statement may take as much room as another, yet a definite statement may be many times as effective. The difference is vast. If a claim is worth making, make it in the most impressive way.

—— Law ——
If a claim is worth making,
make it in the most impressive way.

All these effects must be studied. Salesmanship-in-print is very expensive. A salesman's loose talk matters little. But when you are talking to millions at enormous cost, the weight of your claims is important.

No generality has any weight whatever. It is like saying "How do you do?" When you have no intention of inquiring about one's health. But specific claims when made in print are taken at their value.

—— Law ——
No generality has any weight whatever.

## How to Apply Today

The laws in this chapter are perhaps the most violated laws in modern day advertising. View your promotion and website and see for yourself just how many times you violate these laws. Here's a little test you can do.

## Being Specific

1. Count the *Generalized Statements* ("Guaranteed to work","Great service", "Safe and reliable").

2. Count the *Exaggerations* ("Used the world over","best services","cheapest prices").

3. Now count the *Specific Facts* ("Used in 52 Countries"," Guaranteed to deliver a result in 10 minutes", "52 new safety features").

You could call this your *Believability Score*. Apply this formula:

Specific Facts - General statements - Exaggerations = Believability Score

Anything below zero is not convincing and regarded as false or misleading. A total score above zero indicates you are believable and convincing: the higher the score, the better.

That is a simple test you can perform on any of your promotions.

# 8
## Tell Your Full Story

*"Claims" are statements made about the benefits or performance of a product or service. The term "benefits" is more common today. - Tony*

WHATEVER CLAIM YOU use to gain attention, the advertisement should tell a story reasonably complete. If you watch returns, you will find that certain claims appeal far more than others. But in usual lines a number of claims appeal to a large percentage. Then present those claims in every ad for their effect on that percentage.

## Claims or Benefits

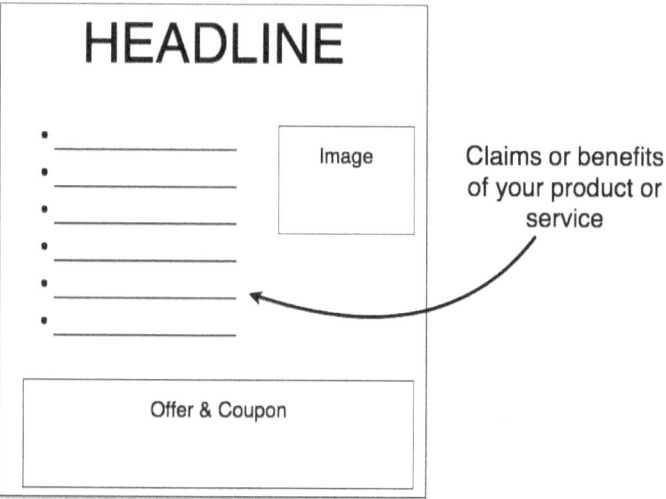

Some advertisers, for sake of brevity (brief, use of little words), present one claim at a time. Or they write a serial ad, continued in another issue. There is no greater folly (foolishness). Those serials almost never connect. (A serial ad is a series of ads where the story or benefits are continued in another ad often published at a different time.)

# Tell Your Full Story

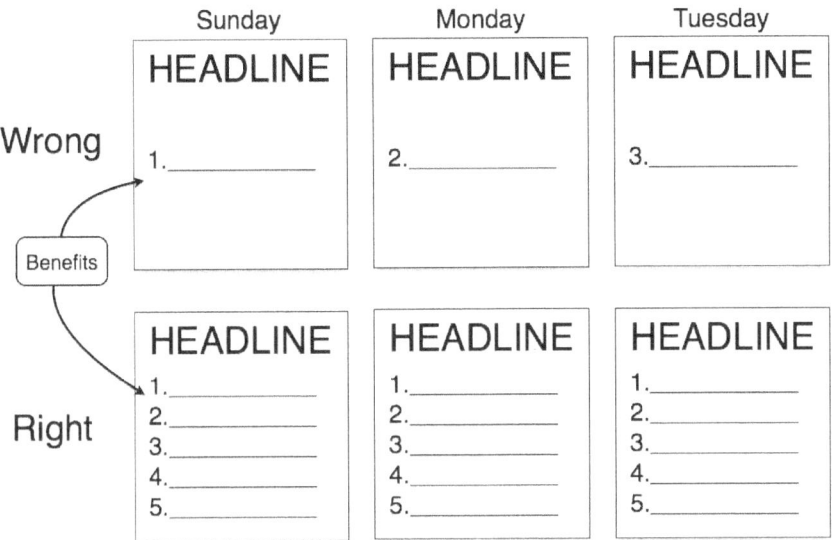

When you once get a person's attention, then is the time to accomplish all you can ever hope with him. Bring all your good arguments to bear. Cover every phase of your subject. One fact appeals to some, one to another. Omit any one and a certain percentage will lose the fact which might convince.

—— Law ——

When you get a person's attention, then is the time to accomplish all you can ever hope with him.

People are not apt to read successive advertisements on any single line (product). No more than you read a news item twice, or a story. In one reading of an advertisement one decides for or against a proposition (offer). And that operates against a second reading. So present to the

# Tell Your Full Story

reader, when once you get him, every important claim you have.

The best advertisers do that. They learn their appealing claims by tests—by comparing results from various headlines. Gradually they accumulate a list of claims important enough to use. All those claims appear in every ad thereafter.

—— LAW ——

*Present to the reader every important claim you have. The best advertisers do that. They learn their appealing claims by tests—by comparing results from various headlines. Gradually they accumulate a list of claims important enough to use. All those claims appear in every ad thereafter.*

The advertisements seem monotonous to the men who read them all. A complete story is always the same. But one must consider that the average reader is only once a reader, probably. And what you fail to tell him in that ad is something he may never know.

Some advertisers go so far as to never change their ads. Single mail order ads often run year after year without diminishing returns. So with some general ads. They are perfected ads, embodying in the best way known all that one has to say. Advertisers do not expect a second reading. Their constant returns come from getting new readers.

In every ad consider only new customers. People using your product are not going to read your ads. They have already read and decided. You might advertise month after month to present users that the product they use is poison, and they would never know it. So never waste one line of your space to say something to present users, unless you can say it in your headlines. Bear in mind always that you address an unconverted prospect.

— LAW —

In every ad consider only new customers
and tell your full story.

Any reader of your ad is interested, else he would not be a reader. You are dealing with someone willing to listen. Then do your level best (as best you can). That reader, if you lose him now, may never again be a reader.

You are like a salesman in a busy man's office. He [the salesman] may have tried again and again to get entree (the right to enter). He may never be admitted again. This is his one chance to get action, and he must employ it to the full.

This brings up the question of brevity (being brief). The most common expression you hear about advertising is that people will not read much. Yet a vast amount of the best paying advertising shows that people do read much. Then they write (request in writing) for a book, perhaps— for added information.

There is a fixed rule on this subject of brevity. One sentence may tell a complete story on a line like chewing gum. It may on an article like Cream of Wheat. But, whether long or short, an advertising story should be reasonably complete.

―― Law ――

Whether long or short, an advertising story should be reasonably complete.

A certain man desired a personal car. He cared little about the price. He wanted a car to take pride in, else he felt he would never drive it. But, being a good business man, he wanted value for his money.

His inclination was towards a Rolls-Royce. He also considered a Pierce-Arrow, a Locomobile and others. But these famous cars offered no information. Their advertisements were very short. Evidently the makers considered it undignified to argue comparative merits.

The Marmon, on the contrary, told a complete story. He read columns and books about it. So he bought a Marmon (see below), and was never sorry. But he afterwards learned facts about another car at nearly three times the price which would have sold him the car had he known them.

Tell Your Full Story

What folly (foolishness) it is to cry a name in a line like

that, plus a few brief generalities. A car may be a lifetime investment. It involves an important expenditure. A man interested enough to buy a car will read a volume (a lot) about it if the volume is interesting.

So with everything. You may be simply trying to change a woman from one breakfast food to another, one tooth paste, or one soap. She is wedded (fixed, dedicated) to what she is using. Perhaps she has used it for years.

You have a hard proposition (task). If you do not believe it, go to her in person and try to make the change. Not to merely buy a first package to please you, but to adopt your brand. A man who once does that at a woman's door won't argue for brief advertisements. He will never again say, "A sentence will do," or a name claim or a boast

Nor will the man who traces his results. Note that brief ads are never keyed (measured). Note that every traced ad tells a complete story, though it takes columns to tell. Never be guided in any way by ads which are untraced.

Never do anything because some uninformed advertiser considers that something right. Never be led in new paths by the blind. Apply to your advertising ordinary common sense. Take the opinion of nobody, the verdict of nobody, who knows nothing about his returns.

—— Law ——

Take the opinion of nobody, the verdict of nobody, who knows nothing about his returns.

## How to Apply Today

Many consider that prospects will not read long letters,

or do not watch long, online videos. The fact is: only those who are interested will read or watch them, and they are the ones you want!

Today there are many useful tools that provide you with insight into the reading and viewing habits of prospects. For instance, it is possible to track what a website visitor clicks on, what pages they scroll and how long they spend on the site (google search for "heat map"). With videos it's now possible to see how much of the video was viewed, if sections were skipped or replayed and where the viewer is geographically, as well as what time they viewed it (google search for "video marketing").

All of this information can be used to further fine tune your message or story and improve your results. Such tools help you apply the last law in this chapter.

# 9
## ART IN ADVERTISING

Pictures in advertising are very expensive. Not in cost of good art work alone, but in the cost of space. From one-third to one-half of an advertising campaign is often staked on the power of the pictures.

Anything expensive must be effective, else it involves much waste. So art in advertising is a study of paramount importance.

Pictures should not be used merely because they are interesting. Or to attract attention. Or to decorate an ad. We have covered these points elsewhere. Ads are not written to interest, please or amuse. You are not writing to please the hoi-polloi (the masses; the common people). You are writing on a serious subject—the subject of money spending. And you address a restricted minority.

—— Law ——
Pictures should not be used merely because they are interesting. Or to attract attention. Or to decorate an ad.

Use pictures only to attract those who may profit you. Use them only when they form a better selling argument than the same amount of space set in type (words).

Use pictures only to attract those who may profit you. Use them only when they form a better selling argument than the same amount of space in written words.

Mail order advertisers, as we have said, have pictures down to a science. Some use large pictures, some small, some omit pictures entirely. A noticeable fact is that none of them uses expensive art work. Be sure that all these things are done for reasons made apparent by results.

Any other advertiser should apply the same principles. Or, if none exist to apply to his line, he should work out his own by tests. It is certainly unwise to spend large sums on a dubious adventure.

Pictures in many lines form a major factor. Omitting the lines [of text] where the article (product) itself should be pictured. In some lines, like Arrow Collars (brand name of a type of man's shirt) and in clothing advertising, pictures have proved most convincing. Not only in picturing the collar or the clothes, but in picturing men whom others envy, in surroundings which others covet (desire to possess). The pictures subtly suggest that these articles of apparel will aid men to those desired positions.

So with correspondence schools. Theirs is traced advertising. Picturing men in high positions of taking upward steps forms a very convincing argument.

So with beauty articles. Picturing beautiful women, admired and attractive, is a supreme inducement. But there is a great advantage in including a fascinated man. Women desire beauty largely because of men. Then show them using their beauty, as women do use it, to gain maximum effect.

Advertising pictures should not be eccentric (strange or unusual). Don't treat your subject lightly. Don't lessen respect for yourself or your article by any attempt at frivolity (silliness). People do not patronize (give financial support to) a clown. There are two things about which men should not joke. One is business, one is home.

An eccentric picture may do you serious damage. One may gain attention by wearing a fool's cap. But he would ruin his selling prospects.

Then a picture which is eccentric or unique takes attention from your subject. You cannot afford to do that. Your main appeal lies in headline. Over-shadow that and you kill it. Don't, to gain general and useless attention, sacrifice the attention that you want.

Don't be like a salesman who wears conspicuous clothes. The small percentage he appeals to are not usually good buyers. The great majority of the sane and thrifty heartily despise him. Be normal in everything you do when you are seeking confidence and conviction.

Generalities cannot be applied to art. There are seeming exceptions to most statements. Each line must be studied by itself.

## Art In Advertising

But the picture must help sell the goods. It should help more than anything else could do in like space, else use that something else.

Many pictures tell a story better than type can do. In advertising of Puffed Grains the picture of the grains were found to be most effective. They awake curiosity. No figure drawing in that case compare in results with these grains.

Other pictures form a total loss. We have cited cases of that kind. The only way to know, as is with most other questions, is by compared results. There are disputed questions in art work which we will cite without expressing opinions. They seem to be answered both ways, according to the line which is advertised.

Does it pay better to use fine art work or ordinary? Some advertisers pay up to $2,000 per drawing. They figure that the space is expensive. The art cost is small in comparison. So they consider the best worth its cost.

Others argue that few people have art education. They bring out their ideas, and bring them out well, at a fraction of the cost. Mail order advertisers are generally in this class.

The question is one of small moment (importance or concern). Certainly good art pays as well as mediocre. And the cost of preparing ads is very small compared with the cost of insertion.

Should every ad have a new picture? Or may a picture be repeated? Both viewpoints have many supporters. The probability is that repetition is an economy. We are after new customers always. It is not probable that they remember a picture we have used before. If they do, repetition does not detract.

Do color pictures pay better than black and white? Not generally, according to the evidence we have gathered to date. Yet there are exceptions. Certain food dishes look far better in colors. Tests on lines like oranges, desserts, etc. show that color pays. Color comes close to placing the products in actual exhibition.

But color used to amuse or to gain attention is like anything else that we use for that purpose. It may attract many times as many people, yet not secure a hearing from as many whom we want.

The general rule applies. Do nothing to merely interest, amuse, or attract. That is not your province (area of interest). Do only that which wins the people you are after in the cheapest possible way.

—— Law ——

Do nothing to merely interest, amuse, or attract.
Do only that which wins the people you are after
in the cheapest possible way.

But these are minor questions. They are mere economies, not largely affecting the results of a campaign.

Some things you do may cut all your results in two. Other things can be done which multiply those results. Minor costs are insignificant when compared with basic principles. One man may do business in a shed, another in a palace. That is immaterial. The great question is, one's power to get the maximum results.

## How to Apply Today

Today pictures or images are inexpensive. The real question is whether an image is better than words? Or does a video produce a better result? You should test all these things.

Generic stock images usually provide no real benefit in terms of response rates. What proves more effective than generic stock images, are images of the business owner or actual clients. Cartoon images (that tell a story) are also effective and should be tested.

There are many ways to get customized images designed or videos created, google search for "art work" or "video marketing." The right image or video can make a dramatic difference to response rates. I highly recommend you try it out.

# 10
## THINGS TOO COSTLY

MANY THINGS ARE possible in advertising which are too costly to attempt. That is another reason why every project and method should be weighed and determined by a known scale of cost and result.

Changing people's habits is very expensive. A project which involves that must be seriously considered. To sell shaving soap to the peasants of Russia one would first need to change their beard wearing habits. The cost would be excessive. Yet countless advertisers try to do things almost as impossible. Just because questions are not ably considered, and results are traced but unknown.

For instance, the advertiser of a dentifrice (toothpaste) may spend much space and money to educate people to brush their teeth. Tests which we know of have indicated that the cost of such converts may run from $20 to $25 each. Not only because of the difficulty, but because much of the advertising goes to people already converted.

Such a cost, of course, is unthinkable. One might not in a lifetime get it back in sales. The maker who learned these facts by tests make no attempt to educate people to the tooth brush habit. What cannot be done on a large scale profitably can not be done on a small scale. So not one line [of text] in any ad is devoted to this object. This maker, who is constantly guided in everything by keying (measuring) every ad, has made remarkable success.

Another dentifrice (toothpaste) maker spends much money to make converts to the tooth brush. The object is commendable, but altruistic (more concerned with others). The new business he creates is shared by his rivals. He is wondering why his sales increase is in no way commensurate (in proportion) with his expenditure.

An advertiser at one time spent much money to educate people to the use of oatmeal. The results were too small to discover. All people know of oatmeal. As a food for children it has age-old fame. Doctors have advised it for many generations. People who don't serve oatmeal are therefore difficult to start. Perhaps their objections are insurmountable. Anyway, the cost proved to be beyond all possible return.

There are many advertisers who know facts like these and concede (accept) them. They would not think of devoting a whole campaign to any such impossible object. Yet they devote a share of their space to that object. That is only the same folly (foolishness) on a smaller scale. It is not good business.

No one orange grower or raisin grower could attempt to increase the consumption of those fruits. The cost might be a thousand times his share of the returns. But thousands of growers combined have done it on those and many other lines. There lies one of the great possibilities of advertising development. The general consumption of scores of foods can be profitably increased. But it must be done on wide

## Things Too Costly

co-operation.

No advertiser could afford to educate people on vitamins or germicides (germ killer, an antiseptic). Such things are done by authorities, through countless columns of unpaid-for space. But great successes have been made by going to people already educated and satisfying their created wants.

It is a very shrewd (cunning, perceptive, intelligent) thing to watch the development of a popular trend, the creation of new desires. Then at the right time offer to satisfy those desires. That was done on yeasts, for instance, and on numerous antiseptics. It can every year be done on new things which some popular fashion or widespread influence is brought into vogue. But it is a very different thing to create that fashion, taste or influence for all in your field to share.

There are some things we know of which might possibly be sold to half the homes in the country. A Dakin-fluid germicide (type of antiseptic, germ killing substance), for instance. But the consumption would be very small. A small bottle might last for years. Customers might cost $1.50 each. And the revenue per customer might not in ten years repay the cost of getting.

Mail order sales on single articles (products), however popular, rarely cost less than $2.50 each. It is reasonable to suppose that sales made through dealers (local retailers) on like articles (products) will cost approximately as much. Those facts must be considered on any one-sale article (product). Possibly one user will win others. But traced returns as in mail order advertising would prohibit much advertising which is now being done.

Costly mistakes are made by blindly following some ill-conceived idea. An article (product), for instance, may have many uses, one of which is to prevent disease. Prevention is not a popular subject, however much it should be. People will do much to cure trouble, but people in general will do little to prevent it. This has been proved by many disappointments.

—— LAW ——
People will do much to cure trouble,
but people in general will do little to prevent it.

One may spend much money in arguing prevention when the same money spent on another claim would bring many times the sales. A heading which asserts one claim may bring ten times the results of a heading which asserted another. An advertiser may go far astray unless he finds out.

A tooth paste may tend to prevent decay. It may also beautify teeth. Tests will probably find that the latter appeal is many times as strong as the former. The most successful tooth paste advertiser never features tooth troubles in his headlines. Tests have proved them unappealing. Other advertisers in this line center on those troubles. That is often because results are not known and compared.

A soap may tend to cure eczema. It may at the same time improve complexion. The eczema claim may appeal to one in a hundred while the beauty claims would appeal to nearly all. To even mention the eczema claims might destroy the beauty claims.

A man has a relief for asthma. It has done so much for him he considers it a great advertising possibility. We have no statistics on this subject. We do not know the percentage of people who suffer from asthma. A canvass (to question people to find their opinion on something) might show it to be one in a hundred. If so, he would need to cover a hundred useless readers to reach one he wants. His cost of result might be twenty times as high as on another article which appeals to one in five. That excessive cost would probably mean disaster. For reasons like these every new advertiser should seek for wise advice. No one with the interests of advertising at heart will advise any dubious venture.

Some claims not popular enough to feature in the main are still popular enough to consider. They influence a certain number of people—say one-fourth of your possible customers. Such claims may be featured to advantage in a certain percentage of headlines. It should probably be included in every advertisement. But those are not things to guess at. They should be decided by actual knowledge, usually by traced returns.

This chapter, like every chapter, points out a very important reason for knowing your results. Scientific advertising is impossible without that. So is safe advertising. So is maximum profit.

Groping in the dark in this field has probably cost enough money to pay the national debt. That is what has filled the advertising graveyards. That is what has discouraged thousands who could profit in this field. And the dawn of knowledge is what is bringing a new day in the advertising world.

## How to Apply Today

Selling a prevention is much harder than selling a cure or something that one desires. Prevention selling requires continuous education to get the prospect motivated to take action. Today, continuous educational promotion can be set up so that a prospect automatically gets the necessary information they need on a regular basis until they make a decision. That was not possible in Claude's day. Of course, all of the laws still apply. You need to tests what type of educational promotion works best: mailed letters, DVDs, online videos, live events, and webinars, to mention a few, are tools you can use to educate your prospects.

However, a prospect with a problem or desire for something that is better, faster or easier already has the motivation to take action now. Therefore, the best results are achieved when a prevention-type product or service is altered and sold as a cure to a problem. That's done by testing different offers and can be very beneficial indeed!

# 11
## INFORMATION

AN AD-WRITER, to have a chance at success, must gain full information on his subject. The library of an ad agency should have books on every line that calls for research. A painstaking advertising man will often read for weeks on some problem which comes up.

—— LAW ——

An ad-writer, to have a chance at success, must gain full information on his subject.

Perhaps in many volumes he will find few facts to use. But some one fact may be the keystone of success.

This writer (Claude Hopkins) has just completed an enormous amount of reading, [on] medical [information] and otherwise [general information], on coffee. This is to advertise a coffee without caffeine. One scientific article out of a thousand perused (read thoroughly or carefully) gave the keynote for that campaign. It was the fact that caffeine stimulation comes two hours after drinking. So the immediate bracing effects which people seek from coffee do not come from the caffeine. Removing caffeine does not remove the kick. It does not modify coffees delights, for caffeine is tasteless and odorless.

Caffeineless coffee has been advertised for years. People regarded it like near-beer (non-alcoholic beer). Only through weeks of reading did we find a way to put it in another light.

To advertise a tooth paste this writer has also read many volumes of scientific matter dry as dust. But in the middle of one volume he found the idea which has helped make millions for that tooth paste maker. And has made this campaign one of the sensations of advertising.

Genius is the art of taking pains (hard work or effort). The advertising man who spares the midnight oil will never get very far.

Before advertising a food product, 130 men were employed for weeks to interview all classes of consumers.

On another line, letters were sent to 12,000 physicians. Questionnaires are often mailed to tens of thousands of men and women to get the viewpoint of consumers.

A $25,000-a-year man, before advertising outfits for acetylene gas (smelly gas which burns with a bright flame, used in welding and formerly in lighting), spent weeks in going from farm to farm. Another man did that on a tractor [before advertising the tractor].

Before advertising a shaving cream, one thousand men were asked to state what they most desired in a shaving soap.

## Information

—— Law ——
Know your client's needs and
desires before you advertise.

Called on to advertise pork and beans, a canvass (survey) was made of some thousand of homes. Theretofore (before then) all pork and bean advertising has been based on "Buy my brand." That canvass showed that only 4 percent of the people used any canned pork and beans. Ninety-six percent baked their beans at home.

The problem was not to sell a particular brand. Any such attempt appealed to only four percent. The right appeal was to win the people away from home-baked beans. The advertising, which without that knowledge must have failed, proved a great success.

A canvass is made, not only of homes, but of dealers (local retailers). Competition is measured up.

Every advertiser of a similar product is written for his literature and claims. Thus we start with exact information on all that our rivals are doing.

Clipping bureaus (a company that reads newspapers and magazines to clip articles and other information from these sources to send to customers who pay for this service) are patronized (visited as a customer), so that everything printed on our subject comes to the man who writes ads.

—— Law ——
Know what the competition is offering and how.

Every comment that comes from consumers or dealers goes to this man's desk.

It is often necessary in a line to learn the total expenditure. We must learn what a user spends a year, else we shall not know if users are worth the cost of getting.

We must learn the total consumption, else we may overspend.

―― LAW ――

We must learn what a user spends a year, else we shall not know if users are worth the cost of getting. We must learn the total consumption, else we may overspend.

We must learn the percentage of readers to whom our product appeals. We must often gather this data on classes. The percentage may differ on farms and in cities. The cost of advertising largely depends on the percentage of waste circulation.

Thus an advertising campaign is usually preceded by a very large volume of data. Even an experimental campaign, for effective experiments cost a great deal of work and time.

## Information

Often chemists are employed to prove or disprove doubtful claims. An advertiser, in all good faith, makes an impressive assertion. If it is true, it will form a big factor in advertising. If untrue, it may prove a boomerang (a negative repercussion). And it may bar our ads from good mediums. It is remarkable how often a maker proves wrong on assertions he had made for years.

Impressive claims are made far more impressive by making them exact. So, many experiments are made to get the actual figures. For instance, a certain drink is known to have a large food value. That simple assertion is not very convincing. So we send the drink to the laboratory and find that its food value is 425 calories per pint. One pint is equal to six eggs in calories of nutriment (nourishment). That claim makes a great impression.

In every line involving scientific details a censor (an official who examines material that is about to be released) is appointed. The ad-writer, however well informed, may draw wrong inferences (conclusions) from facts. So an authority passes on every advertisement.

The uninformed would be staggered to know the amount of work involved in a single ad. Weeks of work sometimes. The ad seems so simple, and it must be simple to appeal to simple people. But back of that ad may lie reams of data, volumes of information, months of research.

So this is no lazy man's field.

## Law

The ad seems so simple, and it must be simple to appeal to simple people. But behind that ad may lie reams of data, volumes of information, months of research.

## How to Apply Today

While clipping bureaus still exist today, *Google Alerts* provides a simple way to keep up to date with any media related to your industry, including what your competition are doing. You can create as many alerts as you want and best of all, it's free! Checkout google.com/alerts.

# 12
## STRATEGY

ADVERTISING IS MUCH like war, minus the venom. Or much, if you prefer, like a game of chess. We are usually out to capture others' citadels (a fortress or city) or garner (gather) others' trade.

We must have skill and knowledge. We must have training and experience, also right equipment. We must have proper ammunition, and enough. We dare not underestimate opponents. Our intelligence department is a vital factor, as told in the previous chapter. We need alliances with dealers (local retailers), as another chapter tells. We also need strategy of the ablest sort, to multiply the value of our forces.

—— LAW ——
We need strategy to multiply the value of our forces.

Sometimes in new campaigns comes the question of a name. That may be most important. Often the right name is an advertisement in itself. It may tell a fairly complete story, like Shredded Wheat, Cream of Wheat, Puffed Rice, Spearmint Gum, Palmolive Soap, etc.

That may be a great advantage. The name is usually

## Strategy

conspicuously displayed. Many a name has proved to be the greatest factor in an articles success. Other names prove a distinct disadvantage—Toasted Corn Flakes, for instance. Too many others may share a demand with the man who builds it up.

Many coined names without meaning have succeeded. Kodak, Karo (syrup), Mazda, etc., are examples. They are exclusive. The advertiser who gives them meaning never needs to share his advantage. But a significant name which helps to impress a dominant claim is certainly a good advantage. Names that tell stores (explain a lot) have been worth millions of dollars. So a great deal of research often precedes the selection of a name.

Sometimes a price must be decided. A high price creates resistance. It tends to limit one's field. The cost of getting an added profit may be more than the profit.

It is a well-known fact that the greatest profits are made on great volume at small profit. Campbell's Soups, Palmolive Soap, Karo Syrup and Ford cars are conspicuous (obvious) examples. A price which appeals only to—say 10 percent [of the population]—multiplies the cost of selling.

—— Law ——

It is a well-known fact that the greatest profits are made on great volume at small profit. A price which appeals only to 10 percent of the population multiplies the cost of selling.

But on other lines high price is unimportant. High profit is essential. The line may have a small sale per customer.

## Strategy

One hardly cares what he pays for a corn (a small, painful area of thickened skin on the foot) remedy because he uses little. The maker must have a large margin because of small consumption.

On other lines a higher price may even be an inducement. Such lines are judged largely by price. A product which costs more than the ordinary is considered above the ordinary. So the price question is always a very big factor in strategy.

—— Law ——
The price question is always a very big factor in strategy.

Competition must be considered. What are the forces against you? What have they in price or quality or claims to weigh against your appeal? What have you to win trade (sales) against them? What have you to hold [that] trade against them when you get it?

How strongly are your rivals entrenched? There are some fields which are almost impregnable (hard to penetrate). They are usually lines which create a new habit or custom and which typify (become associated with) that custom with consumers. They so dominate a field that one can hardly hope to invade it. They have volume, the profit to make a tremendous fight.

Such fields are being constantly invaded. But it is done through some convincing advantage, or through very superior salesmanship-in-print.

Other lines are only less difficult. A new shaving soap, as an example. About every possible customer is using a rival

## Strategy

soap. Most of them are satisfied with it. Many are wedded to it. The appeal must be strong enough to win those people from long-established favor.

Such things are not accomplished by haphazard efforts. Not by considering people in the mass and making blind stabs for their favors (what is liked or meets approval). We must consider individuals, typical people who are using rival brands. A man on a Pullman (a luxurious railroad cabin with with sleeping berths and a bathroom), for instance, using his favorite soap. What could you say to him in person to get him to change to yours? We cannot go after thousands of men until we learn how to win one.

—— Law ——
We cannot go after thousands
until we learn how to win one.

The maker may say that he has no distinctions. He is making a good product, but much like others. He deserves a good share of the trade, but he has nothing exclusive to offer. However, there is nearly always something impressive which others have not told. We must discover it. We must have a seeming advantage. People don't quit habits without reason.

—— Law ——
There is nearly always something impressive
which others have not told. We must discover it.

# Strategy

### —— Law ——
### We must have a seeming advantage.
### People don't quit habits without reason.

There is the problem of substitution (customers buying similar products) and how to head it off. That often steals much of one's trade. This must be considered in ones original plan. One must have foresight to see all eventualities, and the wisdom to establish his defenses in advance.

Many pioneers in the line establish large demands. Then through some fault in their foundations, lose a large share of the harvest. Theirs is a mere brand, for instance, where it might have stood for an exclusive product.

Vaseline is an example. That product established a new demand, then almost monopolized that demand through wisdom at the start. To have called it some different brand of petroleum jelly might have made a difference of millions in results.

Jell-O (brand of Jelly), Postum (coffee substitute), Victrola (type of phonograph, an old record player), Kodak, etc., established coined names which came to typify a product. Some such names have been admitted to the dictionary. They have become common names, though coined and exclusive.

Royal Baking Powder and Toasted Corn Flakes, on the other hand, when they pioneered their fields, left the way open to perpetual substitution. So did Horlick's Malted Milk.

The attitude of dealers must be considered. There is a

growing inclination to limit lines, to avoid duplicate lines, to lesson inventories. If this applies to your line, how will dealers receive it? If there is opposition, how can we circumvent it?

The problems of distribution are important and enormous. To advertise something that few dealers supply is a waste of ammunition. Those problems will be considered in another chapter.

These are samples of the problems which advertising men must solve. These are some of the reasons why vast experience is necessary. One oversight may cost the client millions in the end. One wrong piece of strategy may prohibit success. Things done in one way may be twice as easy, half as costly, as when done another way.

Advertising without this preparation is like a waterfall going to waste. The power might be there, but it is not made effective. We must center the force and direct it in a practical direction.

Advertising often looks very simple. Thousands of men claim ability to do it. And there is still a wide impression that many men can. As a result, much advertising goes by favor (what is liked or meets approval rather than what works). But the men who know realize that the problems are as many and as important as the problems in building a skyscraper. And many of them lie in the foundations.

# 13
## Use of Samples

THE PRODUCT ITSELF should be its own best salesman. Not the product alone, but the product plus a mental impression, and atmosphere, which you place around it. That being so, samples are of prime importance. However expensive, they usually form the cheapest selling method. A salesman might as well go out without his sample case as an advertiser.

—— Law ——

The product plus a mental impression and the atmosphere you place around it is the best salesman.

Sampling does not apply to little things alone, like foods or proprietaries (trademarked products). It can be applied in some way to almost everything. We have sampled clothing. We are now sampling phonograph records.

## Use of Samples

Samples serve numerous valuable purposes. They enable one to use the word "Free" in ads. That often multiplies readers. Most people want to learn about any offered gift. Tests often show that samples pay for themselves—perhaps several times over—in multiplying the readers of your ads without additional cost of space.

Samples enable one to use the word "Free" in ads. That often multiplies readers.

A sample gets action. The reader of your ad may not be convinced to the point of buying. But he is ready to learn more about the product that you offer. So he cuts out a coupon, lays it aside, and later mails it or presents it. Without that coupon he would soon forget.

—— LAW ——

A sample of your product or service gets action.

Then you have the name and address of an interested prospect. You can start him using your product. You can give him fuller (more complete) information. You can follow him up.

—— LAW ——

Through samples (or give-aways) you can collect the contact details of interested prospects allowing you to give them more complete information and follow them up.

That reader might not again read one of your ads in six

## Use of Samples

months. Your impression would be lost. But when he writes you, you have a chance to complete with that prospect all that can be done. In that saving of waste the sample pays for itself.

Sometimes a small sample is not a fair test. Then we may send an order on the dealer (retailer) for a full-size package. Or we may make the coupon good for a package at the store. Thus we get a longer test.

You say that is expensive. So is it expensive to gain a prospects interest. It may cost you 50 cents to get the person to the point of writing for a sample. Don't stop at 15 cents additional to make that interest valuable.

Another way in which samples pay is by keying (identifying and measuring) your advertisements. They register the interest you create. Thus you can compare one with another ad, headline, plan and method.

That means in any line an enormous savings. The wisest, most experienced man cannot tell what will most appeal in any line of copy (text). Without a key to guide you, your returns are very apt to cost you twice what they need cost. And we know that some ads on the same product will cost ten times what others cost. A sample may pay for itself several times over by giving you an accurate check.

Again samples enable you to refer customers where they can be supplied. This is important before you attain general distribution.

Many advertisers lose much by being penny-wise. They are afraid of imposition (costs or burdens), or they try to save pennies. That is why they ask ten cents for a sample,

## Use of Samples

or a stamp or two. Getting that dime may cost them from 40 cents to $1. That is, it may add that to the cost of replies. But it is remarkable how many will pay that addition rather than offer a sample free.

Putting a price on a sample greatly retards replies. Then it prohibits you from using the word "Free," as we have stated, will generally more than pay for your samples.

For the same reason some advertisers say, "You buy one package, we will buy the other." Or they make a coupon good for part of the purchase price. Any keyed returns will clearly prove that such offers do not pay. Before a prospect is converted, it is approximately as hard to get half price for your article as to get the full price for it.

—— LAW ——

Before a prospect is converted, it is just as hard to get half price for your product or service as it is to get the full price.

Bear in mind that you are the seller. You are the one courting (trying to attract) interest. Then don't make it difficult to exhibit that interest. Don't ask your prospects to pay for your selling efforts. Three in four will refuse to pay —perhaps nine in ten.

—— LAW ——

You are the one trying to attract interest.
Then don't make it difficult to exhibit that interest.

## Use of Samples

—— Law ——

Don't ask your prospects to pay for your selling efforts.

Cost of requests for samples differ in every line. It depends on your breadth of appeal. Some things appeal to everybody, some to a small percentage. One issue of the papers in Greater New York brought 1,460,000 requests for a can of evaporated milk. On a chocolate drink, one-fifth the coupons published are presented. Another line not widely used may bring a fraction of that number.

But the cost of inquiries is usually enough to be important. Then don't neglect them. Don't stint (restrict) your efforts with those you have half sold. An inquiry means that a prospect has read your story and is interested. He or she would like to try your product and learn more about it. Do what you would do if that prospect stood before you.

Cost of inquiries depends largely on how they come. Asking people to mail the coupon brings minimum returns. Often four times as many will present that coupon for a sample at the store.

On a [product] line before the writer now, sample inquiries obtained by mail average 70 cents each. The same ads bring inquiries at from 18 cents to 22 cents each when the coupons are presented at a local store.

## Use of Samples

Most people write few letters. Writing is an effort. Perhaps they have no stamps in the house. Most people will pay carfare (fare for travel on public transportation) to get a sample rather than two cents postage. Therefore, it is always best, where possible, to have samples delivered locally.

On one line three methods were offered. The woman could write for a sample, or telephone, or call at a store. Seventy percent of the inquiries came by telephone. The use of the telephone is more common and convenient than the use of stamps.

***Note from Tony:*** *The above result shows that the most convenient methods—the telephone—produced the best results. Today,*

## Use of Samples

*making such offers available online, via a website, would provide the most convenient method. However, it depends on your type of client and would require testing. The best approach is having multiple ways for a client to make contact, as summarized by the following law:*

—— Law ——

Make it easy for your customer—easy to order, easy to pay, easy to collect, easy to use, easy to access and easy to understand.

Sometimes it is not possible to supply all dealers (local retailers) with samples. Then we refer people to some central stores. These stores are glad to have many people come there. And other dealers do not generally object so long as they share in the sales.

It is important to have these dealers send you the coupons promptly. Then you can follow up the inquiries while their interest is fresh.

It is said that sample users repeat (use more than one sample). They do to some extent. But repeaters form a small percentage. Figure it in your cost.

Say to the woman, "Only one sample to a home" and few women will try to get more of them. And the few who cheat you are not generally the people who would buy. So you are not losing purchasers, but the samples only.

—— Law ——

Say, "Only one sample to a home" and few will try to get more of them. And the few who cheat you are not

## Use of Samples

generally the people who would buy. So you are not losing purchasers, but the samples only.

On numerous lines we have for long offered full-sized packages free. The packages were priced at from 10 cents to 50 cents each. In certain territories for a time we have checked up on repeaters. And we found the loss much less than the cost of checking.

In some lines samples would be wasted on children, and they are most apt to get them. Then say in your coupon "adults only." Children will not present such coupons, and they will rarely mail them in.

But one must be careful about publishing coupons good for a full-size package at any store. Some people, and even dealers, may buy up many papers. We do not announce the date of such offers. And we insert them in Sunday papers, not so easily bought up.

But we do not advocate samples given out promiscuously. Samples distributed to homes, like waifs (abandoned pet) on the doorsteps, probably never pay. Many of them never reach the house or the housewife. When they do, there is no prediction for them. The product is cheapened. It is not introduced in a favorable way.

So with demonstrations in stores. There is always a way to get the same results at a fraction of the cost.

Many advertisers do not understand this. They supply thousands of samples to dealers to be handed out as they will. Could a trace be placed on the cost of returns, the

## Use of Samples

advertiser would be stunned.

Give samples to interested people only. Give them only to people who exhibit that interest by some effort. Give them only to people whom you have told your story. First create an atmosphere of respect, a desire, an expectation. When people are in that mood, your sample will usually confirm the qualities you claim.

—— LAW ——

Give samples to interested people only. Give them only to people who exhibit that interest by some effort. Give them only to people whom you have told your story. First create an atmosphere of respect, a desire, an expectation. When people are in that mood, your sample will usually confirm the qualities you claim.

Here again comes the advantage of figuring cost per customer. That is the only way to gauge advertising. Samples sometimes seem to double advertising cost. They often cost more than the advertising. Yet, rightly used, they almost invariably form the cheapest way to get customers. And that is what you want.

The argument against samples are usually biased. They may come from advertising agents who like to see all the advertising money spent in print. Answer such arguments by tests. Try some towns with them, some without. Where samples are effectively employed, we rarely find a line where they do not lessen the cost per customer.

## How to Apply Today

We call samples either "gifts" or "bribes" (we bribe the

## Use of Samples

prospect with a reward for giving us their details.)

Today you can give away ebooks, audio books, checklists and videos, all of which cost little or nothing to create and nothing to deliver. Free online events like webinars are a fantastic way to build a contact list.

When providing free live events or physical products (sent by mail), don't say it's free and simply give it away. First get the prospect to claim their free ticket or a free voucher that has a value (like $59). Then make them present the voucher before sending the gift or allowing entry to the live event.

Google search for "online forms" to find apps you can use to add forms to your website that collect contact details and provide numbered vouchers or tickets.

# 14
## Getting Distribution

Most advertisers are confronted with the problem of getting distribution. National advertising is unthinkable without that. A venture cannot be profitable if nine in ten of the converts fail to find the goods.

To force dealers (local retailers) to stock by bringing repeated demands may be enormously expensive. To cover the country with a selling force is usually impossible. To get dealers to stock an unknown line on promise of advertising is not easy. They have seen too many efforts fail, too many promises rescinded (cancelled).

## Distribution Methods

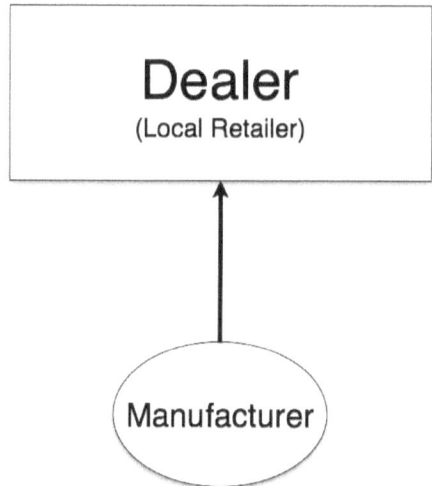

We cannot discuss all plans for getting distribution. There are scores (lots) of ways employed, according to the enterprise. Some start by soliciting direct sales—mail orders—until the volume of demand forces dealers to supply.

Some get in touch with prospects by a sample or other offer, then refer them to certain dealers who are stocked.

## Getting Distribution

Some well-known lines can get a large percentage of dealers to stock in advance under guarantee of sale. Some consign goods to jobbers (wholesalers) so dealers can easily order. Some name certain dealers in their ads until dealers in general stock.

### Distribution Methods

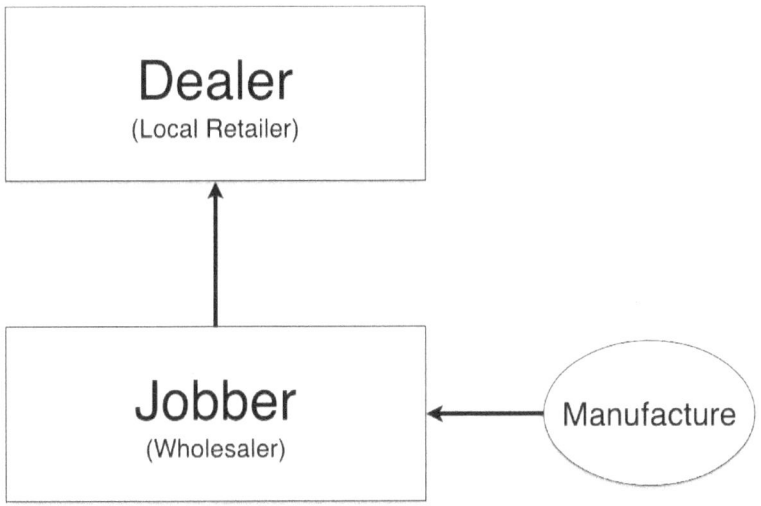

The problems in this line are numberless. The successful methods are many. But most of them apply to lines too few to be worthy of discussion in a book like this.

We shall deal here with articles (products) of wide appeal and repeated sales, like foods or proprietary (trademarked) articles.

## Getting Distribution

We usually start with local advertising, even though magazine advertising is best adapted to the article (product). We get our distribution town by town, then change to national advertising.

— Law —

Start with local advertising, even though another medium is best adapted to the article (product). We get our distribution town by town, then change to national advertising.

Sometimes we name the dealers who are stocked. As others stock, we add their names. When a local campaign is proposed, naming certain dealers, the average dealer wants to be included. It is often possible to get most of them by offering to name them in the first few ads.

Whether you advertise few or many dealers, the others will stock in very short order if the advertising is successful. Then the trade is referred to all dealers.

The sample plans dealt with in the previous chapter aid quick distribution. They often pay for themselves in this way alone.

If the samples are distributed locally, the coupon names the store. The prospects who go there to get the samples know that those stores are supplied, if a nearer dealer is not. Thus little trade is lost.

When sample inquiries come to the advertiser, inquiries are referred to certain dealers at the start. Enough demand is centered there to force those dealers to supply it.

Sometimes most stores are supplied with samples, but

## Getting Distribution

on the requirement of a certain purchase. You supply a dozen samples with a dozen packages, for instance. Then inquiries for samples are referred to all stores. This quickly forces general distribution. Dealers don't like to have their customers go to competitors even for a sample.

Where a coupon is used, good at any store for a full-size package, the problem of distribution becomes simple. Mail to dealers proofs of the ad which will contain a coupon. Point out to each that many of his customers are bound to present that coupon. Each coupon represents a cash sale at full profit. No average dealer will let those coupon customers go elsewhere.

Such a free-package offer often pays for itself in this way. It forms the cheapest way of getting general distribution.

Some of the most successful advertisers have done this in a national way. They have inserted coupon ads in magazines, each coupon good at any store for a full-size package. A proof of the ad is sent to dealers in advance, with a list of the magazines to be used, and their circulation.

In this way, in one week sometimes, makers attain a reasonable national distribution. And the coupon ad, when it appears, completes it. Here again the free packages cost less than other ways of forcing distribution. And they start thousands of users besides. Palmolive Soap and Puffed Grains are among the products which attain their distribution in that way.

Half the circulation of a newspaper may go to outside towns. That half may be wasted if you offer a sample at

## Getting Distribution

local stores. Say in your coupon that outside people should write you for a sample. When they write, do not mail the sample. Send the samples to a local store, and refer inquiries to that store. Mailing a sample may make a convert who cannot be supplied. But the store which supplies the sample will usually supply [future] demand.

In these ways, many advertisers get national distribution without employing a single salesman. They get it immediately. And they get it at far lower cost than by any other method.

There are advertisers who, in starting, send every dealer a few packages as a gift. That is better, perhaps, than losing customers created. But it is very expensive. Those free packages must be sold by advertising. Figure their cost at your selling price, and you will see that you are paying a high cost per dealer. A salesman might sell these small stocks at a lower cost. And other methods might be vastly cheaper.

Sending stocks on consignment to retailers is not widely favored. Many dealers resent it. Collections are difficult. And non-businesslike methods do not win dealer respect.

The plans advocated here are the best plans yet discovered for the lines to which they apply. Other lines require different methods. The ramifications are too many to discuss in a book like this.

But don't start advertising without distribution. Don't get distribution by methods too expensive. Or by slow, old-fashioned methods. The loss of time may cost you enormously in sales. And it may enable energetic rivals to get ahead of you.

—— Law ——

Don't start advertising without distribution.
Don't get distribution by methods too expensive.

Go to men who know by countless experiences the best plan to apply to your line.

## How to Apply Today

Thankfully distribution is much easier today!

Drop shipping is a service in which the seller does not keep goods in stock, but sends the order details to the manufacturer or wholesaler, who then ships the goods directly to the customer. It is also called a fulfillment service.

The fulfillment service can be notified automatically of every new order by email. The email contains all the necessary information to send the product to the client. The seller pays for the cost of handling and shipping.

Amazon provides a worldwide fulfillment service and there are many smaller organizations that do so. Google "fulfillment services" to find one.

## On Demand Services

For those of you who publish books, DVDs, CDs or

manuals, you can use an On Demand Publishing service.

A new order for the item (book, DVD, CD, etc.) it is printed or created and mailed. Again, notification can happen automatically via email. You'll be surprised that the quality of on-demand services has reached the same (if not better) quality than producing large quantities of such items.

On-demand services provide a huge cost saving as no money is tied up in stocking or storing such items. You only incur costs when an item sells. Google "On Demand (Books, DVDs, CDs, etc.)"

With fulfillment services and on-demand printing, the last Law stated in this chapter can easily be followed!

# 15
## TEST CAMPAIGNS

ALMOST ANY QUESTION can be answered, cheaply, quickly and finally, by a test campaign. And that's the way to answer them—not by arguments around a table. Go to the court of last resort (the final court of appeal where judgment is made, used figuratively)—the buyers of your product.

—— LAW ——

Almost any question can be answered, cheaply, quickly and finally, by a test campaign.
And that's the way to answer them—not by arguments around a table.

On every new project there comes up the question of selling that article profitably. You and your friends may like it, but the majority may not. Some rival product may be better liked or cheaper. It may be strongly entrenched. The users won away from it may cost too much to get.

## Test Campaigns

People may buy and not repeat. The article may last too long. It may appeal to a small percentage, so most of your advertising goes to waste.

There are many surprises in advertising. A project you will laugh at may make a great success. A project you are sure of may fall down. All because tastes differ so. None of us know enough peoples desires to get an average viewpoint.

### Law
None of us know enough peoples desires
to get an average viewpoint.

In the old days, advertisers ventured on their own opinions. The few guess right, the many wrong. Those were the times of advertising disaster. Even those who succeeded came close to the verge (edge) before the tide was turned (direction changed). They did not know their cost per customer or their sale per customer. The cost of selling might take a long time to come back. Often it never came back.

Now we let the thousands decide what the millions will do. We make a small venture (a test with unknown results, a risk), and watch cost and result. When we learn what a thousand customers cost, we know almost exactly what a million will cost. When we learn what they buy, we know what a million will buy.

### Law
In the old days advertisers used their own opinions.
They did not know their cost per customer or their sale

## Test Campaigns

per customer. Now we let the thousands decide what the millions will do. We test small and watch cost and result.

We establish averages on a small scale, and those averages always hold. We know our cost, we know our sale, we know our profit and loss. We know how soon our cost comes back. Before we spread out, we prove our undertaking absolutely safe. So there are today no advertising disasters piloted (tested) by men who know.

—— LAW ——

We establish averages on a small scale, and those averages always hold. We know our cost, we know our sale, we know our profit and loss. We know how soon our cost comes back. Before we spread out, we prove our undertaking absolutely safe.

Perhaps we try out our project in four or five towns. We may use a sample offer or a free package to get users started quickly. Then we wait and see if users buy those samples. If they do, will they continue? How much will they buy? How long does it take for the profit to return our cost of selling?

A test like this may cost $3,000 to $5,000. It is not all lost, even when the product proves unpopular. Some sales are made. Nearly every test will in time bring back the entire cost.

Sometimes we find that the cost of the advertising comes back before the bills are due. That means that the product can be advertised without investment. Many a great advertiser has been built up without any cost whatever beyond immediate receipts (costs). That is an ideal situation.

Sometimes we find that the cost of the advertising comes back before the bills are due. That means that the product can be advertised without investment. Many a great advertiser has been built up without any cost. That is an ideal situation.

On another product it may take three months to bring back the cost with a profit. But one is sure of his profit in that time. When he spreads out he must finance accordingly.

Think what this means. A man has what he considers an advertising possibility. But national advertising looks so big and expensive that he dare not undertake it.

Now he presents it in a few average towns, at a very moderate cost. With almost no risk whatever. From the few thousand he learns what the millions will do. Then he acts accordingly. If he then branches (expands the activity) he knows to a certainty just what his results will be.

He is playing on the safe side of a hundred to one shot. If the article (product) is successful, it may make him millions. If he is mistaken about it, the loss is a trifle (thing of little value or importance).

These are facts we desire to emphasize and spread. All our largest accounts are now built in this way, from very small beginnings. When business men realize that this can be done, hundreds of others will do it. For countless fortune-earners now lie dormant.

The largest advertiser in the world makes a business of starting such projects. One by one he finds out winners. Now he has twenty-six, and together they earn many millions yearly.

These test campaigns have other purposes. They answer countless questions which arise in business.

A large food advertiser felt that his product would be more popular in another form. He and all his advisers were certain about it. They were willing to act on this supposition without consulting the consumers, but wiser advice prevailed.

He inserted an ad in a few towns with a coupon, good at any store for a package of the new-style product. Then he wrote to the users about it. They were almost unanimous in their disapproval.

Later the same product was suggested in still another form. The previous verdict made the change look dubious. The advertiser hardly thought a test to be worth while. But he submitted the question to a few thousand women in a similar way and 91 percent voted for it. Now he has a unique product which promises to largely increase his sales.

These tests cost about $1,000 each. The first one saved him a very costly mistake. The second will probably bring him large profits.

Then we try test campaigns to try out new methods on

advertising already successful. Thus we constantly seek for better methods, without interrupting plans already proved out.

We try test campaigns to try out new methods on advertising already successful. Thus we constantly seek for better methods, without interrupting plans already proven.

In five years for one food advertiser we tried out over fifty separate plans. Every little while we found an improvement, so the results of our advertising constantly grew. At the end of five years we found the best plan of all. It reduced our cost of selling by 75 percent. That is, it was four times more effective than the best plan used before.

That is what mail order advertisers do—try out plan after plan to constantly reduce the cost. Why should any general advertiser be less business-like and careful?

Another service of the test campaign is this:

An advertiser is doing mediocre advertising. A skilled advertising agent feels that he can greatly increase results. The advertiser is doubtful. He is doing fairly well. He has alliances which he hesitates to break. So he is inclined to let well enough alone.

Now the question can be submitted to the verdict of a test. The new agent may take a few towns, without interfering with the general campaign. Then compare his results with the general results and prove his greater skill.

Plausible arguments are easy in this line. One man after

another comes to an advertiser to claim superior knowledge or ability. It is hard to decide, and decisions may be wrong.

Now actual figures gained at a small cost can settle the question definitely. The advertiser makes no commitment. It is like saying to a salesman, "Go out for a week and prove yourself." A large percentage of all the advertising done would change hands if this method were applied.

Again we come back to scientific advertising. Suppose a chemist would say in an arbitrary way that this compound was best, or that better. You would little respect his opinion. He makes tests—sometimes hundreds of tests—to actually know which is best. He will never state a supposition (belief or idea) before he has proved it. How long before advertisers in general will apply that exactness to advertising?

## How to Apply Today

You don't need an ad agency to test for you. It can be done easily today using online advertising platforms like Google Adwords or Facebook Advertising (as mentioned in my closing comments in *Headline* chapter).

The only additional comment worth stating is this: testing requires dedication, imagination and initiative. The motivations of individuals, fads and trends are constantly changing and a good marketer never stops trying to improve on last week's performance. The game is no different today than it was in Claude's day. It's just faster, bigger and, I believe, more fun. We can reach the world from a laptop, sell goods shipped from China to people in Australia while sitting on the beach in the Bahamas.

Claude would no doubt consider it miraculous. But he would probably have worked just as hard.

# 16
## LEANING ON DEALERS

*FROM THE TONE of this chapter, you can assume that getting local retailer's to stock goods in Claude's time was not an easy task. Thankfully today we have fulfillment services (as discussed in the "Distribution" chapter). However, there are some key laws in this chapter that still apply today. - Tony*

WE CANNOT DEPEND much in most lines on the active help of jobbers (wholesalers) or of dealers (local retailers). They are busy. They have many lines to consider. The profit on advertised lines is not generally large. And an advertised article is apt to be sold at cut prices.

The average dealer does what you would do. He exerts himself on brands of his own, if at all. Not on another mans brand.

## Leaning On Dealers

The dealers will often try to make you think otherwise. He will ask [for] some aid (help) or concession (additional benefits) on the ground of extra effort. Advertisers often give extra discounts. Or they make loading offers—perhaps one case free in ten—in the belief that loaded dealers will make extra efforts.

This may be so in rare lines, but not generally. And the efforts if made do not usually increase the total sales. They merely swing trade from one store to another.

On most lines, making a sale without making a convert does not count for much. Sales made by conviction—by advertising—are likely to bring permanent customers. People who buy through casual recommendations do not often stick. Next time someone else gives other advice.

—— LAW ——

Making a sale without making a convert does not count for much. Sales made by conviction—by advertising—are likely to bring permanent customers.

Revenue which belongs to the advertiser is often given away without adequate return. These discounts and gifts could be far better spent in securing new customers.

Free goods must be sold, and by your efforts usually. One extra case with ten means that advertising must sell ten percent more to bring you the same return. The dealer would probably buy just as much if you let him buy as convenient (easily).

Much money is often frittered (wasted) away on other forms of dealer help. Perhaps on window or store displays.

## Leaning On Dealers

A window display, acting as a reminder, may bring to one dealer a lions share of the trade. Yet it may not increase your total sales at all.

Those are facts to find out. Try one town in one way, one in another. Compare total sales in those towns. In many lines such tests will show that costly displays are worthless. A growing number of experienced advertisers spend no money on displays.

—— Law ——

Tests will show that costly displays are worthless. A growing number of experienced advertisers spend no money on displays.

This is all in line (the subject) of general publicity, so popular long ago. Casting bread upon the waters and hoping for its return (a biblical saying implying that a person will ultimately benefit from their good deeds without any additional effort). Most advertising was of that sort twenty years ago.

Now we put things to the test. We compare cost and result on every form of expenditure. It is very easily done. Very many costly wastes are eliminated by this modern process.

—— Law ——

Now we put things to the test. We compare cost and result on every form of expenditure. It is very easily done.

Scientific advertising has altered many old plans and

conceptions. It has proved many long established methods to be folly (foolish). And why should we not apply to these things the same criterion we apply to other forms of selling? Or to manufacturing costs?

Your object in all advertising is to buy new customers at a price which pays a profit. You have no interest in garnering (gathering) trade at any particular store. Learn what your consumers cost and what they buy. If they cost you one dollar each, figure that every wasted dollar costs you a possible customer.

—— LAW ——

Your object in all advertising is to buy new customers at a price which pays a profit.

—— LAW ——

Learn what your consumers cost and what they buy. If they cost you one dollar each, figure that every wasted dollar costs you a possible customer.

Your business will be built in that way, not by dealer help. You must do your own selling, make your own success. Be content if dealers fill the orders that you bring. Eliminate your wastes. Spend all your ammunition where it counts for most.

—— LAW ——

You must do your own selling,
make your own success.

# 17

## Individuality

A PERSON WHO desires to make an impression must stand out in some way. Being eccentric, being abnormal is not distinction to covet (desire or crave). But doing admirable things in a different way gives one a great advantage.

—— Law ——
A person who desires to make an impression
must stand out in some way.

—— Law ——
Doing admirable things in a different way
gives one a great advantage.

So with salesmen, in person or in print. There is uniqueness which belittles and arouses resentment. [Alternatively] there is refreshing uniqueness which enhances, which we welcome and remember. Fortunate is the salesman who has it.

We try to give each advertiser a becoming (flattering) style. We make him distinctive, perhaps not in appearance, but in manner and in tone. He is given an individuality

## Individuality

best suited to the people he addresses.

One man appears rugged and honest in a line where rugged honesty counts. One may be a good fellow where choice is a matter of favor. In other lines the man stands out by impressing himself as an authority.

We have already cited a case where a woman made a great success in selling clothing to girls, solely through a created personality which won.

That's why we have signed ads sometimes—to give them a personal authority. A man is talking—a man who takes pride in his accomplishments—not a "soulless corporation." Whenever possible we introduce a personality into our ads. By making a man famous we make his product famous. When we claim an improvement, naming the man who made it adds effect.

—— Law ——

Whenever possible we introduce a personality into our ads. By making a person famous we make their product famous. When we claim an improvement, naming the person who made it adds effect.

Then we take care not to change an individuality which has proved appealing. Before a man writes a new ad on that line, he gets into the spirit adopted by the advertiser. He plays a part as an actor plays it.

—— Law ——

We take care not to change an individuality which has proved appealing. Before a man writes a new ad he gets

## Individuality

into the spirit adopted by the advertiser. He plays a part as an actor plays it.

In successful advertising great pains (lots of effort or work) are taken to never change our tone. That which won so many is probably the best way to win others. Then people come to know us. We build on that acquaintance rather than introduce a stranger in guise. People do not know us by name alone, but by looks and mannerisms. Appearing different every time we meet never builds up confidence.

### Law
In successful advertising we never change our tone. Appearing different every time we meet never builds up confidence.

Then we don't want people to think that salesmanship is made to order. That our appeals are created, studied, artificial. They must seem to come from the heart, and the same heart always, save where a wrong tack (approach) forces a complete change.

There are winning personalities in ads as well as people. To some we are glad to listen, others bore us. Some are refreshing, some commonplace. Some inspire confidence, some caution.

To create the right individuality is a supreme accomplishment. Then an advertiser's growing reputation on that line brings him ever-increasing prestige. Never weary of that part. Remember that a change in our characteristics would compel our best friends to get acquainted all over.

## How to Apply Today

These laws on individuality are applied today through the use of celebrities to endorse a product or company.

It is easier than you think to hire a celebrity and not as costly as you may assume. Google search for "hire a celebrity."

Another alternative is to add your personality to your company, product or service. Richard Branson did this and it helped develop the *Virgin* brand into one known for it's fun, exciting and "try-anything" culture.

Of course, all of these things should be tested. And when choosing a personality to endorse your brand keep in mind your ideal customer and test small first. You never know, you might end up a being more effective than a celebrity!

# 18
## NEGATIVE ADVERTISING

TO ATTACK A rival is never good advertising. Don't point out others' faults. It is not permitted in the best mediums. It is never good policy. The selfish purpose is apparent. It looks unfair, not sporty. If you abhor knockers, always appear a good fellow.

——— LAW ———

To attack a rival is never good advertising.
Don't point out others' faults. It is never good policy.

Show the bright side, the happy and attractive side, not the dark and uninviting side of things. Show beauty, not homeliness (unattractiveness); health, not sickness. Don't show the wrinkles you propose to remove, but the face as it will appear. Your customers know all about wrinkles.

——— LAW ———

Show the bright side, the happy and attractive side, not the dark and uninviting side of things. Show beauty, not ugliness; health, not sickness. Don't show the wrinkles you propose to remove, but the face as it will

# Negative Advertising

appear. Your customers know all about wrinkles.

In advertising a dentifrice (toothpaste), show pretty teeth, not bad teeth. Talk of coming good conditions, not conditions which exist. In advertising clothes, picture well-dressed people, not the shabby. Picture successful men, not failures, when you advertise a business course. Picture what others wish to be, not what they may be now.

We are attracted by sunshine, beauty, happiness, health, success. Then point the way to them, not the way out of the opposite.

Picture envied people, not the envious.

Tell people what to do, not what to avoid.

―― LAW ――
Tell people what to do, not what to avoid.

Make your every ad breathe good cheer. We always dodge a Lugubrious Blue. (*Lugubrious* means looking or sounding sad and *Blue* refers to a sad mood. The term *Lugubrious Blue* comes from a comic strip of the 1920 entitled *Mr Lugubrious Blue and Mr Simely Gladd*. Mr Blue always focused on the negative side whereas Mr Gladd looked at the bright side. Hence *"dodge a Lugubrious Blue"* means to avoid something negative and depressing.)

Assume that people will do what you ask. Say, "Send now for this sample." Don't say, "Why do you neglect this offer?" That suggests that people are neglecting. Invite them to follow the crowd.

## Negative Advertising

—— Law ——
Assume that people will do what you ask.
Invite them to follow the crowd.

Compare the results of two ads, one negative, one positive. One presenting the dark side, one the bright side. One warning, the other inviting. You will be surprised. You will find that the positive ad out pulls the other four to one, if you have our experience.

—— Law ——
You will find that the positive ad out pulls the other four to one, if you have our experience.

The "Before and after taking" ads are follies (foolish acts) of the past. They never had a place save with the afflicted. Never let their memory lead you to picture the gloomy side of things.

—— Law ——
The "Before and after taking" ads are foolish acts of the past.

## How to Apply Today

As a side note, I find Claude's comments regarding the use of "Before and After" photos in advertising very interesting. The weight-loss industry has thrived on the use of such negative advertising. But I can't help but wonder what a test campaign might produce?

## **Call-to-Action**

Every ad and promotion piece must have a call to action. State exactly what the prospect must do next. Here are some examples:

1. Call 9999 9999 Now
2. Click here to download ...
3. Enter Your Details Below to get your free ...

Some online marketers claim that the use of arrows has improved response rates. For example use arrows to point directly to a form the prospect needs to complete or to a button they need to click. Such things need testing. But one thing is certain—tell them what to do and in long letters or videos tell them more than once!

# 19
# Letter Writing

THIS IS ANOTHER phase of advertising which all of us have to consider. It enters, or should enter, into all campaigns. Every business man receives a large number of circular letters. Most of them go direct to the waste basket. But he acts on others, and others are filed for reference.

—— Law ——
Letter writing should be included in all campaigns.

Analyze those letters. The ones you act on or the ones you keep have a headline which attracted your interest. At a glance they offer something that you want, something you may wish to know.

Remember that point in all advertising.

A certain buyer [for a corporation] spends $50,000,000 per year. Every letter, every circular which comes to his desk gets its deserved attention. He wants information on the [product] lines he buys.

But we have often watched him. In one minute a score of letters may drop into the waste basket. Then one is laid aside. That is something to consider at once. Another is

## Letter Writing

filed under the heading "Varnish." And later when he buys varnish that letter will turn up.

That buyer won several prizes by articles [written] on good buying. His articles were based on information. Yet the great masses of matter which came to him never got more than a glance.

The same principles apply to all advertising. Letter writers overlook them just as advertisers do. They fail to get the right attention. They fail to tell what buyers wish to know.

One magazine sends out millions of letters annually. Some to get subscriptions, some to sell books. Before the publisher sends out five million letters he puts a few thousands to test. He may try twenty-five letters, each with a thousand prospects. He learns what results will cost. Perhaps the plan is abandoned because it appears unprofitable. If not, the letter which pays best is the letter that he uses.

Just as men are doing now in all scientific advertising.

Mail order advertisers do likewise. They test their letters as they test their ads. A general letter is never used until it proves itself best among many actual returns.

Letter writing has much to do with advertising. Letters to inquirers, follow-up letters. Wherever possible they should be tested. Where that is not possible, they should be based on knowledge gained by tests.

—— LAW ——
Letter writing has much to do with advertising.

# Letter Writing

Letters to inquirers, follow-up letters.
Wherever possible they should be tested.

We find the same difference in letters as in ads. Some get action, some do not. Some complete a sale, some forfeit the impression gained. These letters, going usually to half-made converts, are tremendously important.

Experience generally shows that a two-cent letter gets no more attention than a one-cent letter. Fine stationery no more than poor stationery. The whole appeal lies in the matter (content).

It has been found that fine stationery and pamphlets lessen the effect. They indicate an effort to sell on other lines (other methods) than merit. That has the same effect in letters as in ads.

—— Law ——

It has been found that fine stationery and pamphlets lessen the effect. They indicate an effort to sell on other methods than merit. That has the same effect in letters as in ads.

A letter which goes to an inquirer is like a salesman going to an interested prospect. You know what created that interest. Then follow it up along that line, not on some different argument. Complete the impression already created. Don't undertake another guess.

# Letter Writing

In a letter as in ads, the point is to get immediate action. People are naturally dilatory (slow to act). They postpone, and a postponed action is too often forgotten.

—— LAW ——

In a letter, as in ads, the point is to get immediate action. People are naturally slow to act. They postpone, and a postponed action is too often forgotten.

Do something if possible to get immediate action. Offer some inducement for it. Or tell what delay may cost. Note how many successful selling letters place a limit on an offer. It expires on a certain date. That is all done to get prompt decision, to overcome the tendency to delay.

—— LAW ——

Do something if possible to get immediate action. Offer some inducement for it. Or tell what delay may cost. Note how many successful selling letters place a limit on an offer. It expires on a certain date. That is all done to get prompt decision, to overcome the tendency to delay.

A mail order advertiser offered a catalog. The inquirer might send for three or four similar catalogs. He had that competition in making a sale.

So he wrote a letter when he sent his catalog, and enclosed a personal card. He said, "You are a new customer, and we want to make you welcome. So when you send your order please enclose this card. The writer wants to see that you get a gift with order— something you can keep."

With an old customer he gave some other reason for the gift. The offer aroused curiosity. It gave preference to his catalog. Without some compelling reason for ordering elsewhere, the woman sent the order to him. The gift paid for itself several times over by bringing larger sales per catalog.

The ways for getting action are many. Rarely can one way be applied to two lines. But the principles are universal. Strike while the iron is hot. Get a decision then. Have it followed by prompt action when you can.

—— Law ——

Strike while the iron is hot. Get a decision then.
Have it followed by prompt action when you can.

You can afford to pay for prompt action rather than lose by delay. One advertiser induced hundreds of thousands of women to buy six packages of his product and send him the trademarks (cut outs of the product label), to secure a premium offer good only for one week.

## How to Apply Today

Your gift or bribe starts the selling process. That process must be mapped out and clearly defined. Test and improve each step of the process. That is what we do. The selling process should include all forms of communication: emails, texting, mailed letters and phone calls. And today the process can be totally automated.

Different methods can be tested to see what encourages the prospect closer to the sale. Higher priced items often require longer selling process.

# Prediction

Once you have built your sales process, you can then accurately predict sales as illustrated below.

Here is the scientific, surefire way to selling. With a predictable sales process, your business is worth a fortune and truly turns your business into a money making machine.

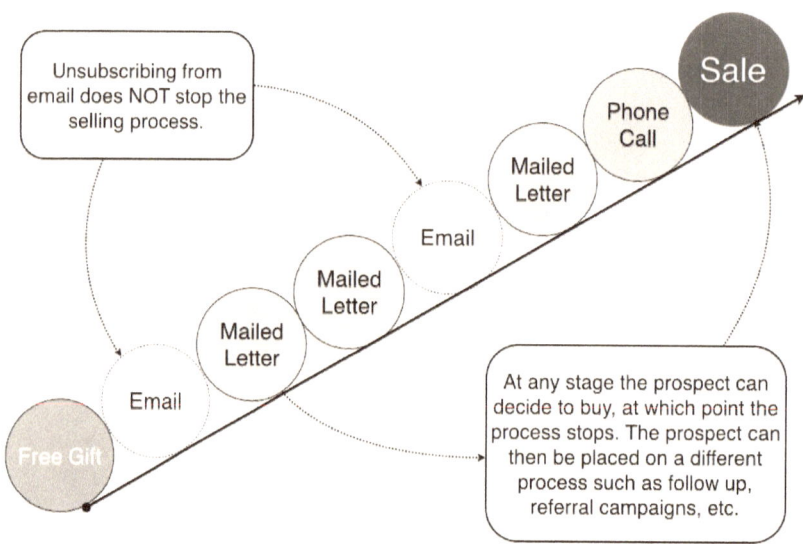

## Letter Writing

# Predictable Selling

# 20
# A Name That Helps

THERE IS GREAT advantage in a name that tells a story. The name is usually prominently displayed. To justify the space it occupies, it should aid the advertising. Some such names are almost complete advertisements in themselves. May Breath (candy for bad breath) is such a name. Cream of Wheat is another. That name alone has been worth a fortune. Other examples are Dutch Cleanser, Cuticura (skincare product), Dynashine (shoe polish), Minute Tapioca (cake mix, now part of the Kraft Brand), 3-in-One Oil, Holeproof (clothing brand), Alcorub (sterilizing gel made from alcohol), etc.

Such names may be protected, yet the name itself describes the product, so it makes a valuable display.

Other coined names are meaningless. Some examples are Kodak, Karo (syrup), Mazda, Sapolio (soap), Vaseline, Kotex (feminine care products), Lux (soap), Postum (coffee substitute), etc. They can be protected, and long-continued advertising may give them a meaning. When this is accomplished they become very valuable. But the great majority of them never attain status.

Such names do not aid the advertising. It is very

doubtful that they justify display. The service of the product, not the name, is the important thing in advertising. A vast amount of space is wasted in displaying names and pictures which tell no selling story. The tendency of modern advertising is to eliminate waste.

The service of the product, not the name, is the important thing in advertising.

A vast amount of space is wasted in displaying names and pictures which tell no selling story. The tendency of modern advertising is to eliminate waste.

Other coined names signify ingredients which anyone may use. Examples are Syrup of Figs, Coconut Oil Shampoo, Tar Soap, Palmolive Soap, etc.

Such products may dominate a market if the price is reasonable, but they must to a degree meet competition. They invite substitution. They are naturally classified with other products which have like ingredients, so the price must remain in that class.

# A Name That Helps

Toasted Corn Flakes and Malted Milk are examples of unfortunate names. In each of those cases one advertiser created a new demand. When the demand was created, others shared it because they could use the name. The originators depended only on a brand. It is interesting to speculate on how much more profitable a coined name might have been.

On a patented product it must be remembered that the right to a name expires with that patent. Names like Castoria (laxative), Aspirin, Shredded Wheat Biscuit, etc., have become common property.

This is a very serious point to consider. It often makes a patent an undesirable protection.

Another serious fault in coined names is frivolity (silly, not serious). In seeking uniqueness one gets something trivial. And that is a fatal handicap in a serious product. It almost prohibits respect.

When a product must be called by a common name, the best auxiliary (supporting) name is a man's name. It is much better than a coined name, for it shows that some man is proud of his creation.

—— Law ——

When a product must be called by a common name, the best auxiliary (supporting) name is an individual's name. It is much better than a coined name, for it Shows that a person is proud of their creation.

Thus the question of a name is of serious importance in laying the foundations of a new undertaking. Some names have become the chief factors in success. Some have lost for their originators four-fifths of the trade they developed.

# 21
## Good Business

A rapid stream ran by the writer's boyhood home. The stream turned a wooden wheel and the wheel ran a mill. Under that primitive method, all but a fraction of the streams potentiality went to waste.

Then someone applied scientific methods to that stream—put in a turbine and dynamos (a generator). Now, with no more water, no more power, it runs a large manufacturing plant.

We think of that stream when we see wasted advertising power. And we see it everywhere—hundreds of examples. Enormous potentialities—millions of circulation—used to turn a mill wheel. While others use that same power with manifold (multiple) effect.

We see countless ads running year after year which we know to be unprofitable. Men spending five dollars to do what one dollar might do. Men getting back 30 percent of their cost when they might get 150 percent. And the facts could be easily proved.

We see wasted space, frivolity (silliness), clever conceits (fancy expressions), entertainment. Costly pages filled with palaver (pointless discussion) which, if employed by a salesman, would reflect on his sanity. But those ads are always unkeyed (not traced or measured). The money is spent blindly, merely to satisfy some advertising whim.

Not new advertisers only. Many an old advertiser has little or no idea of his advertising results. The business is growing through many efforts combined, and advertising is given its share of the credit.

An advertiser of many years' standing (long duration), spending as high as $700,000 per year, told the writer he did not know whether his advertising was worth anything or not. Sometimes he thought that his business would be just as large without it.

The writer replied, "I do know. Your advertising is utterly unprofitable, and I could prove it to you next week. End an ad with an offer to pay five dollars to anyone who writes you that he read the ad through. The scarcity of replies will amaze you."

Think what a confession—that millions of dollars being spent without knowledge of results. Such a policy applied to all factors in a business would bring ruin in short order (quickly).

You see other ads which you may not like as well. They may seem crowded or verbose (more words than needed). They are not attractive to you, for you are seeking something to admire, something to entertain. But you will note that those ads are keyed. The probability is that out of scores of traced ads the type which you see has paid the best.

Many other ads which are not keyed now were keyed at the beginning. They are based on known statistics. They won on a small scale before they ever ran on large scale. Those advertisers are utilizing their enormous powers in full.

Advertising is prima facie (is assumed) evidence that the man who pays believes that [all] advertising is good. It has brought great results to others, it must be good for him. So he takes it like some secret tonic which others have endorsed. If the business thrives, the tonic gets credit. Otherwise, the failure is due to fate.

That seems almost unbelievable. Even a storekeeper who inserts a twenty-dollar ad knows whether it pays or not. Every line of a big store's ad is charged to the proper department. And every inch used must the next day justify its cost.

Yet most national advertising is done without justification. It is merely presumed to pay. A little test might show a way to multiply returns.

—— Law ——

Most national advertising is done without justification. It is merely presumed to pay. A little test might show a way to multiply returns.

Such methods, still so prevalent, are not very far from their end. The advertising men who practice them see the writing on the wall. The time is fast coming when men who spend money are going to know what they get. Good business and efficiency will be applied to advertising. Men and methods will be measured by the known returns, and only competent men can survive.

Only one hour ago an old advertising man said to the writer, "The day for our type is done. Bunk (nonsense) has lost its power. Sophistry (falsehoods or use of misleading arguments) is being displaced by actuality. And I tremble at the trend."

So do hundreds tremble. Enormous advertising is being done along scientific lines. Its success is common knowledge. Advertisers along other lines will not much longer be content.

We who can meet the test welcome these changed conditions. Advertisers will multiply when they see that advertising can be safe and sure. Small expenditures made on a guess will grow to big ones on a certainty. Our line of business will be finer, cleaner, when the gamble is removed. And we shall be prouder of it when we are judged on merit.

—— LAW ——

The time is fast coming when men who spend money are going to know what they get. Advertisers will multiply when they see thatadvertising can be safe and sure.

# Part Two:
# Scientific Advertising Applied Today

# 22
## Websites

An effective website has three major functions:

1. List Building
2. Education
3. Public Relations (PR)

You'll discover that a website with all three aligns with many of the laws in this book. Let's explore each in more detail.

## Components of an Effective Website

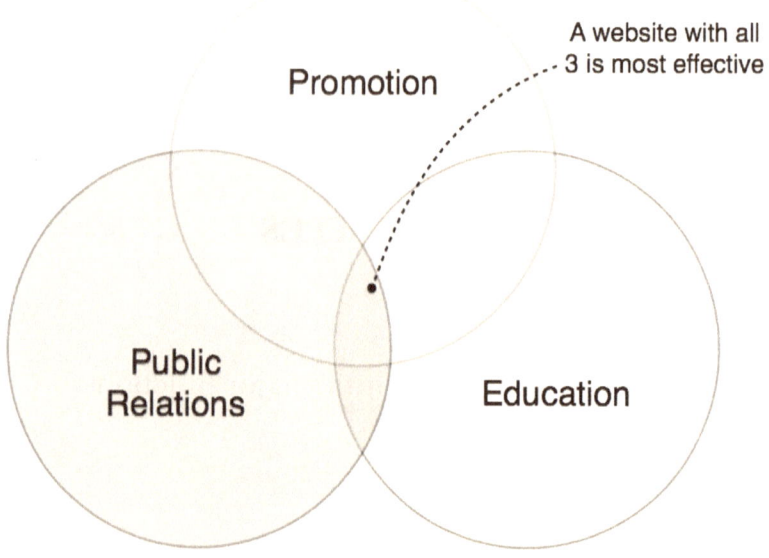

## Promotion

By "list building" we mean building your mailing list which includes the contact details of prospective clients who are interested in your product and services. The first and most important function of your website is to build your list. The best way is to offer a free gift. It follows then that your website should, as a priority, promote your free gifts and make it easy for visitors to get them. Your free gifts should be prominent on every page, in a column and at the top of the page.

When designing websites, follow these guidelines:

## Websites

1. Keep your site free of distractions and moving graphics.

2. Keep menu links simple and too a minimum. Put marketing-type links in the top menu (such as links to free gifts and contacts details).

3. Put links to legal notices and other non-promotional pages in a footer menu.

4. NEVER put ads on your site that take the prospect away to another site, it is a direct violation of the purpose of your website. You want to drive business IN, not drive it away. Every effort should be made to get your visitors to come to your site and enter their contact details. The commissions made from placing ads on your site are small in comparison to the profits you can generate from a well thought out marketing plan.

5. If your sales process requires that people call you then prominently display your phone number and make sure it is a hyperlinked, so when it is clicked on, it will initiate a call. Especially useful for those visitors browsing via a smartphone.

6. If your sales process requires clients visit your premises, display your address with a link to Google Maps, to make it easy for clients to find your location.

7. Ensure your site is mobile friendly. Web browsing via smartphones and tablets is increasing with the trend likely to continue. Your site should be "responsive" which means it will automatically adjust itself to a mobile version of your site which is

easier to navigate via a smartphone or tablet.

8. Ensure all forms that visitors complete are mobile friendly and easy to use. Users abandon forms that are hard to fill out on a cell phone. Test the forms yourself on all devices.

9. Test your website using the most common browsers on different computers—Chrome, Internet Explorer, Firefox and Safari— to ensure it works well with each.

10. Use a tracking system to monitor visitors to your site so you can easily get statistical data such as number of visitors, where they came from and what pages they are viewing; this is vital data to track, it can be used to test headlines and campaigns.

The above list ensures that your site aligns with the laws in this book.

## **Education**

Educating your clients is one of the best ways to promote your products and services. It also makes you an authority on the subject when you provide useful information. A website that educates its visitors will naturally follow many of the laws covered by the chapters *Salesmanship*, *Service* and *Psychology*.

It also solves the problem of Search Engine Optimization (SEO) which is made overly and unnecessarily complex. Below are some simple guiding rules you should follow to achieve effective SEO.

Firstly the basics: The word "blog" come from the term "web log." The word "log" refers to an ongoing record of updates or changes to something. A "blog" is a series of articles posted on a website. These articles can be categorized and tagged.

Google is constantly making a copy of every web page on the internet, including how an article is categorized or tagged. Google tries to find the most relevant web page for users, and therein lies *the* key to successful **SEO**: *being relevant* which also happens to align with many of the laws in this book, specifically:

> The entire return from an ad depends on attracting the right sort of readers.

> The reason for most of the non-successes in advertising is trying to sell people what they do not want.

Google, in their wisdom, is trying to deliver the most relevant information to the user. Knowing this provides you with a very simple 3-step formula for success.

You must ensure your blog contains:

1. Relevant content
2. Regular content
3. Relative location

When you publish educational information, Google and other search engines will help your prospects find that information and lead them to your site.

If your business has geographical limits, it's worth adding your location to the content of your blog posts. For example, mention your city or the suburbs where you conduct business.

By educating your prospects, you are also applying the law:

The more you tell the more you sell.

Think of your blog as your own newspaper. You are the writer, editor and publisher. You can write what you want and Google will help bring you readers. There are some other more technical things that you can do, but these are add-on features that first require the implementation of the 3 "Rs" mentioned above.

## Using Videos

When posting videos on your blog, I recommend including a transcription of the video in the blog post. Google cannot search video content, but it will search the text of your post. It is not very expensive to do; I use upwork.com to find people who can transcribe for me.

## Public Relations (PR)

One of the definitions of PR is to "maintain a favorable public image." This definition describes another function of your site. A favorable public image is achieved by sharing your results. You need to tell the world what a wonderful job you do. The best way is by using Case Studies of your clients. Case Studies are more than just a testimonials; they are an in-depth view of how you helped a client.

You can do this in many ways. There are three types of Case Studies:

1. An interview with a client.
2. A discussion about a specific client *without* the client present.
3. A general discussion of your results *without* naming a specific client.

An interview with a client can range from a professionally filmed interview, to one done via Skype, or a simply a recorded phone call (more on how to record video on your computer in the next chapter).

If using methods 1 or 2 above you will need the client's written permission to use their name. If you are short on time and want to get some promotion live on your site, use method 3. You can do any of the above with little or no cost.

I suggest you add Case Studies articles to your blog and categorize them as "case studies."

Also, as a final point on websites, it's a good idea to submit your site to the search engines. This increases the likelihood of been "found," just google "search engine submission" to find out how.

# 23
## Landing Pages

A Landing Page is a dedicated website page that new a prospect is sent to when they click on an ad. The prospect "lands" on your landing page. Such pages are completely distraction free and have only one purpose—to get the visitor to enter their contact details by offering something for free. They offer only one thing. There are no menu links. Usually, the only external link is to legal notices (such as privacy policy).

## Website Structure

Your main website is like a newspaper that publishes new and interesting (and educational) articles every week. Your landing pages are like salesmen that hit the streets looking for new business. You want ONE newspaper and THOUSANDS of salesmen.

## Landing Pages

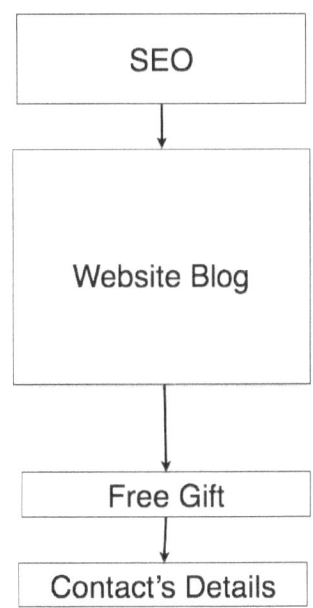

Landing pages ("salesmen") provide you with a constant stream of useful information that help you attract more prospects, reducing the cost per response and cost per sale.

Landing pages are your testing ground. They provide new topics for the blog ("newspaper").

In the chapter *How Advertising Laws Are Established*, I introduced the concept of Split Testings where a different version of the same landing page is automatically shown to the next visitor. Landing Pages are automatically keyed (using Claude's term) which makes them an extremely powerful tool for the marketer. Applying the laws relating to testing can be done with ease.

## Ads & Landing Pages

Normally a visitor is driven to a landing page from an online ad. Let's use Google Ads as an example but keep in mind these concepts also apply to other online advertisers such as Facebook Ads, Twitter, etc.

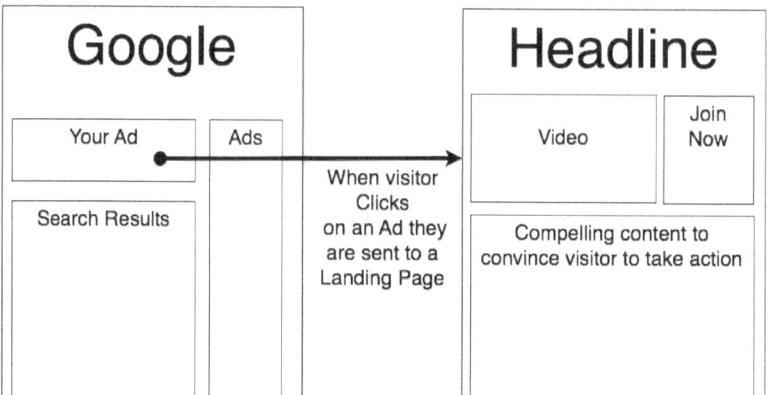

Today, online advertisers ensure that your landing page is relevant to your ad. If your ad is promoting "shoes" let's say, then the word "shoe" and other related words such as "feet," "walking", etc., are expected to be on your landing page. In fact, Google will penalize an advertiser whose landing page lacks relevancy by charging more for an ad click. Likewise, they reward advertisers who have higher relevancy with lower ad costs. (If you want to learn more about how google track relevancy, search for "Google PageRank").

## Summary

Online advertising combined with the split testing of different landing pages creates the ultimate laboratory for the Scientific Marketer, who can create a truly magnificent money making machine.

# 24

## Video Marketing

With modern technology providing more affordable filming equipment and fast internet speeds, video is becoming the cheapest and easiest way to advertise.

Many musicians have used YouTube to catapult themselves to worldwide popularity and success with little or no marketing costs. The music video *Gangnam Style*, for example, has been watched over 2 billion times and has created international fame for the artist.

And it's not just the music industry that has benefited.

Gary Vaynerchuk created *WineLibraryTV.com*, a simple blog with videos of Gary reviewing wines.

This website transformed his father's small wine shop from a $4 million-a-year business to a $50 million-a-year enterprise that makes half of its sales through online orders. In addition to that, he signed a million dollar deal for his first book, *Crush It*! If you visit WineLibraryTV.com you'll see that Gary still uses a simple video recorder to film his wine reviews.

Another business success story is *Orabrush*. A simple

device that helps eliminates bad breath by scraping the tongue. It was a completely rejected product initially, but the inventor Dr. Bob Wagstaff went to the aid of college students. One in particular came up with the idea of creating YouTube videos to market the product. Collectively their videos have been seen over 45 million times. They have sold millions of Orabrushes and have distribution around the world. All created initially from YouTube. Check it out at orabrush.com

Another great example is *Dollar Shave Club*. which is taking on the big players in the men's razor industry. Co-founders Mike Dubin and Mark Levine decided to create a club that men could join which would send new razors every month. They very cleverly positioned the Club as a fun, cheaper and more convenient alternative to buying expensive razors at a store. Their youtube videos have been viewed over 24 million times. Check out dollarshaveclub.com.

Using my personal experience, I have used videos to sell large consulting packages ranging from $15,000 to $40,000. It was simply a matter of sending an interested prospect to a landing page, and then having a salesperson follow them up. Every potential client objection was addressed in the video, and all the salesperson had to do was persist. If someone watched the 30 minute video, we knew they were interested. The conversion rate was very high. Also, it meant that clients heard the "sales pitch" directly from me and could do so at any time they pleased. That made it very easy for them to get the information they needed to make an informed decision. And I was able to add additional information to the video, to help overcome common objections that came up during the sales process.

## Contradicting the Laws

When you watch some of the videos from the examples above you'll see that they are entertaining and quite funny which appears to contradict some of the Laws, namely:

> In advertising there is no useless talk. There is no attempt at entertainment. There is nothing to amuse.

Let me clarify—these are not ads like in Claude's day. Video, like TV, has a natural entertainment aspect to it.

What is more important, however, is the cost of a new client. Making a video and putting it online costs very little making it easy for the campaign to be profitable.

What video allows you to do is engage the client more. In Claude's day, advertising space was limited and costly; print media still is. But with online videos, you are not restricted by space or costs—you can afford to add entertainment and add humor *when it is part of your story, positioning and is relevant to your audience.*

You don't need to be an actor either. Videos can be made very easily, without a video camera. You can create what is called a screencast—a recording of your computer screen and voice. For example, you can record a powerpoint presentation (your screen) along with your voice. I have created most of my videos this way. I do it this way usually because it's faster and easier to put together than filming a live video.

Software for this is not very expensive either. Google search "video editing software" and "screencast software".

When making videos follow these laws:

- The more you tell, the more you sell.
- People are naturally interested in a product or service when they know more about it and understand it.
- Always maintain rapport with your customers.
- When you get a person's attention, then is the time to accomplish all you can ever hope with him.
- Specific facts, when stated, have their full weight and effect.
- If a claim is worth making, make it in the most impressive way.
- Present to the reader every important claim you have. The best advertisers do that. They learn their appealing claims by tests—by comparing results from various headlines. Gradually they accumulate a list of claims important enough to use. All those claims appear in every ad thereafter.
- In every ad consider only new customers and tell your full story.
- Whether long or short, an advertising story should be reasonably complete.

- There is nearly always something impressive which others have not told. We must discover it.

- Tell people what to do, not what to avoid.

- Do something if possible to get immediate action. Offer some inducement for it. Or tell what delay may cost. Note how many successful selling letters place a limit on an offer. It expires on a certain date. That is all done to get prompt decision, to overcome the tendency to delay.

## Summary

Videos are a great, affordable way to get your message out there, to demonstrate your products and services and to make yourself more broadly known. I suggest you give it a try.

# 25
# 114 Profitable Laws of Advertising & Marketing

The 114 Laws apply to different aspects of your marketing campaigns, starting with the Fundamentals that apply to all campaigns, extending to Headlines, Human Nature, the use of Stories and more—in total there are seventeen distinct categories. I hope you revisit this chapter whenever you are creating a campaign, to ensure you are apply each Law. This chapter could also be used as a tool to evaluate existing campaigns, providing clarity on why it worked, and why it didn't.

This chapter is truly priceless, I hope you treasure it as much as I do.

## Fundamental Laws

1. The time has come when advertising has in some hands reached the status of a science. It is based on fixed principles and is reasonably exact.

2. The compass of accurate knowledge directs the shortest, safest, cheapest course to any destination.

3. The cost per reply and cost per dollar of sale show up with utter exactness.

4. We offer a sample, a book, a free package, or something to induce direct replies.

5. Our final conclusions are always based on cost per customer or cost per dollar of sale.

6. We test everything pertaining to advertising.

7. No wise advertiser will ever depart from these fundamental unvarying laws.

## The Laws On Strategy

1. An ad-writer, to have a chance at success, must gain full information on his subject.

2. Know your client's needs and desires before you advertise.

3. Know what the competition is offering and how.

4. We must learn what a user spends a year, else we shall not know if users are worth the cost of getting. We must learn the total consumption, else we may overspend.

5. The ad seems so simple, and it must be simple to appeal to simple people. But behind that ad may lie reams of data, volumes of information, months of research.

6. We need strategy to multiply the value of our forces.

7. It is a well-known fact that the greatest profits are made on great volume at small profit. A price which appeals only to 10 percent of the population multiplies the cost of selling.

8. The price question is always a very big factor in strategy.

9. We cannot go after thousands until we learn how to win one.

10. There is nearly always something impressive which others have not told. We must discover it.

11. We must have a seeming advantage. People don't quit habits without reason.

## The Laws On Salesmanship

1. The only purpose of advertising is to make sales.

2. Advertising is not for general effect. It is not to keep your name before the people.

3. There is one simple way to answer many advertising questions. Ask yourself, "Would it help a salesman sell the goods?" "Would it help me sell them if I met a buyer in person?" A fair answer to those questions avoids countless mistakes.

4. Consider them as prospects standing before you, seeking for information. Give them enough to get action.

5. When you plan or prepare an advertisement, keep before you a typical buyer and be guided by what

you would do if you met the buyer face-to-face.

6. Don't think of people in the mass. That gives you a blurred view. Think of a typical individual, man or woman, who is likely to want what you sell.

7. Before advertising first sell your product or service one-on-one to discover reactions and develop different forms of approach.

8. Send out questionnaires to learn the attitude of the buyers.

9. The advertising man studies the consumer. He tries to place himself in the position of the buyer. His success largely depends on doing that to the exclusion of everything else.

10. The reason for most of the non-successes in advertising is trying to sell people what they do not want.

11. Making a sale without making a convert does not count for much. Sales made by conviction—by advertising—are likely to bring permanent customers.

12. Tests will show that costly displays are worthless. A growing number of experienced advertisers spend no money on displays.

13. You must do your own selling, make your own success.

## The Laws On Testing

1. Take the opinion of nobody, the verdict of nobody,

who knows nothing about his returns.

2. Almost any question can be answered, cheaply, quickly and finally, by a test campaign. And that's the way to answer them—not by arguments around a table.

3. None of us know enough peoples desires to get an average viewpoint.

4. In the old days advertisers used their own opinions. They did not know their cost per customer or their sale per customer. Now we let the thousands decide what the millions will do. We test small and watch cost and result.

5. We establish averages on a small scale, and those averages always hold. We know our cost, we know our sale, we know our profit and loss. We know how soon our cost comes back. Before we spread out, we prove our undertaking absolutely safe.

6. Sometimes we find that the cost of the advertising comes back before the bills are due. That means that the product can be advertised without investment. Many a great advertiser has been built up without any cost. That is an ideal situation.

7. We try test campaigns to try out new methods on advertising already successful. Thus we constantly seek for better methods, without interrupting plans already proven.

8. Now we put things to the test. We compare cost and result on every form of expenditure. It is very easily done.

9. Your object in all advertising is to buy new customers at a price which pays a profit.

10. Learn what your consumers cost and what they buy. If they cost you one dollar each, figure that every wasted dollar costs you a possible customer.

11. Most national advertising is done without justification. It is merely presumed to pay. A little test might show a way to multiply returns.

12. The time is fast coming when men who spend money are going to know what they get. Advertisers will multiply when they see that advertising can be safe and sure.

## The Laws On Headlines

1. The purpose of a headline is to pick out people you can interest.

2. What you have will interest certain people only, and for certain reasons. You care only for those people.

3. We pick out what we wish to read by headlines, and we don't want those headlines misleading.

4. Always bear these facts in mind. People are hurried. The average person worth cultivating has too much to read. They skip three-fourths of the reading matter which they pay to get. They are not going to read your business talk unless you make it worth their while and let the headline show it.

5. People will not be bored in print or online.

6. The entire return from an ad depends on attracting the right sort of readers.

7. It is not uncommon for a change in headlines to multiply returns from five or ten times over.

8. Don't think that those millions will read your ads to find out if your product interests. They will decide at a glance—by your headline or your pictures. Address the people you seek, and them only.

## The Laws On Samples & Gifts

1. The product plus a mental impression and the atmosphere you place around it is the best salesman.

2. Samples enable one to use the word "Free" in ads. That often multiplies readers.

3. A sample of your product or service gets action.

4. Through samples (or give-aways) you can collect the contact details of interested prospects allowing you to give them more complete information and follow them up.

5. Before a prospect is converted, it is as hard to get half price for your article as to get the full price for

it.

6. You are the one trying to attract interest. Then don't make it difficult to exhibit that interest.

7. Don't ask your prospects to pay for your selling efforts.

8. Make it easy for your customer—easy to order, easy to pay, easy to collect, easy to use, easy to access and easy to understand.

9. Say, "Only one sample to a home" and few will try to get more of them. And the few who cheat you are not generally the people who would buy. So you are not losing purchasers, but the samples only.

10. Give samples to interested people only. Give them only to people who exhibit that interest by some effort. Give them only to people whom you have told your story. First create an atmosphere of respect, a desire, an expectation. When people are in that mood, your sample will usually confirm the qualities you claim.

## The Laws On Call-to-Action

1. Do something if possible to get immediate action. Offer some inducement for it. Or tell what delay may cost. Note how many successful selling letters place a limit on an offer. It expires on a certain date. That is all done to get prompt decision, to overcome the tendency to delay.

2. Strike while the iron is hot. Get a decision then. Have it followed by prompt action when you can.

## The Laws On Human Nature

1. Remember the people you address are selfish, as we all are. They care nothing about your interests or profit. They seek service for themselves.

2. The best ads ask no one to buy. The ads are based entirely on service. They offer wanted information. They mention advantages to users. Perhaps they offer a sample, or to buy the first package, or to send something on approval, so the customer may prove the claims without any cost or risks.

3. People can be coaxed but not driven. Whatever they do they do to please themselves. Fewer mistakes would be made in advertising if these facts were never forgotten.

4. We learn that curiosity is one of the strongest human incentives.

5. We learn that cheapness is not a strong appeal. People want bargains not cheapness.

6. We learn that people judge largely by price and admire expensive items or service.

7. When the actual cost of something is promoted, that can impress and attract attention and respect.

8. Personalization of communication and products often improves response.

9. An offer limited to a certain class of people is far

more effective than a general offer to everyone.

10. Those who are entitled to any seeming (apparent) advantage will go a long way not to lose that advantage.

11. Providing the customer with a way to purchase something for free (such as a voucher) is more effective than giving it away for free.

12. People are naturally interested in a product or service when they know more about it and understand it.

13. Always maintain rapport with your customers.

14. An identical offer made in a different way may bring multiplied returns.

15. People will do much to cure trouble, but people in general will do little to prevent it.

## The Laws On Ads-in-Print

1. In advertising there is no waste space. Every line is utilized.

2. In advertising there is no useless talk. There is no attempt at entertainment. There is nothing to amuse.

3. In advertising the pictures are always to the point. They are salesmen in themselves. They the earn space they occupy.

4. The more you tell the more you sell.

5. We compare the results of one ad with another. Whenever we do we invariably find that the nearer

we get to proven mail order copy the more customers we get for our money.

## The Laws On Being Specific

1. 1. Exaggerations are usually damaging. They suggest looseness of expression, a tendency to exaggerate, a careless truth. They lead readers to discount all the statements that you make.

2. Specific facts, when stated, have their full weight and effect.

3. If a claim is worth making, make it in the most impressive way.

4. No generality has any weight whatever.

## The Laws On Stories

1. When you get a person's attention, then is the time to accomplish all you can ever hope with him.

2. Present to the reader every important claim you have. The best advertisers do that. They learn their appealing claims by tests—by comparing results from various headlines. Gradually they accumulate a list of claims important enough to use. All those claims appear in every ad thereafter.

3. In every ad consider only new customers and tell your full story.

4. Whether long or short, an advertising story should be reasonably complete.

## The Laws On Art

1. Pictures should not be used merely because they are

interesting. Or to attract attention. Or to decorate an ad.

2. Use pictures only to attract those who may profit you. Use them only when they form a better selling argument than the same amount of space in written words.

3. Do nothing to merely interest, amuse, or attract. Do only that which wins the people you are after in the cheapest possible way.

## The Laws On Distribution

1. Start with local advertising, even though another medium is best adapted to the article (product). We get our distribution town by town, then change to national advertising.

2. Don't start advertising without distribution. Don't get distribution by methods too expensive.

## The Laws On Individuality

1. A person who desires to make an impression must stand out in some way.

2. Doing admirable things in a different way gives one a great advantage.

3. Whenever possible we introduce a personality into our ads. By making a person famous we make their product famous. When we claim an improvement, naming the person who made it adds effect.

4. We take care not to change an individuality which has proved appealing. Before a man writes a new ad he gets into the spirit adopted by the advertiser. He

plays a part as an actor plays it.

5. In successful advertising we never change our tone. Appearing different every time we meet never builds up confidence.

## The Laws On Negative Advertising

1. To attack a rival is never good advertising. Don't point out others' faults. It is never good policy.

2. Show the bright side, the happy and attractive side, not the dark and uninviting side of things. Show beauty, not ugliness; health, not sickness. Don't show the wrinkles you propose to remove, but the face as it will appear. Your customers know all about wrinkles.

3. Tell people what to do, not what to avoid.

4. Assume that people will do what you ask. Invite them to follow the crowd.

5. You will find that the positive ad out pulls the other four to one, if you have our experience.

6. The "Before and after taking" ads are foolish acts of the past.

## The Laws On Letter Writing

1. Letter writing should be included in all campaigns.

2. Letter writing has much to do with advertising. Letters to inquirers, follow-up letters. Wherever possible they should be tested.

3. It has been found that fine stationery and pamphlets lessen the effect. They indicate an effort to sell on

other methods than merit. That has the same effect in letters as in ads.

4. In a letter, as in ads, the point is to get immediate action. People are naturally slow to act. They postpone, and a postponed action is too often forgotten.

## The Laws On Branding

1. The service of the product, not the name, is the important thing in advertising.

2. A vast amount of space is wasted in displaying names and pictures which tell no selling story. The tendency of modern advertising is to eliminate waste.

3. When a product must be called by a common name, the best auxiliary (supporting) name an individual's name. It is much better than a coined name, for it shows that a person is proud of their creation.

# 26
## About Tony

Tony Melvin was born in England and moved to Australian at the age of 8 (with his parents of course).

His entrepreneurial spirit manifested around the age of 10 with his first "enterprise"— it was a car washing business. His younger sister and friend were the hired help. Tony was the salesman. Despite the business having only one client and lasting only a single day, he never forgot how easy it was to make money solving people's problems.

Today, Tony works with a select number of clients as well as trying his hand at fiction writing.

To find out more about Tony or to get in touch visit:

tonymelvin.com

www.ingramcontent.com/pod-product-compliance
Lightning Source LLC
Chambersburg PA
CBHW021424170526
45164CB00001B/87